DISCARDED W9-AEE-127

DATE			
FEB 5 '81			
MAY 27 '81			
NOV 1 8 1987			
FEB 05 '90			
MAR 11 '91			
FEB 24 1995			

© THE BAKER & TAYLOR CO.

Aging
Is a
Family Affair

Aging
Is a
Family Affair

Victoria E. Bumagin
Kathryn F. Hirn

Thomas Y. Crowell, Publishers
New York   Established 1834

This book is dedicated to our children: Louisa, Thomas, Adam, and Neil Hellegers; Deborah and Michael Millman; Susan and Jennifer Bumagin; Peter, Paul, and Jennifer Hirn, who hold forth the promise of joyous old age,

and

in memory of our daughters Elizabeth Alexandra Bumagin and Gretchen Louise Hirn, who were denied such promise.

AGING IS A FAMILY AFFAIR. COPYRIGHT © 1979 by Victoria E. Bumagin and Kathryn F. Hirn. All rights reserved. Printed in the United States of America. No part of this book may be used or reproduced in any manner whatsoever without written permission except in the case of brief quotations embodied in critical articles and reviews. For information address Thomas Y. Crowell, Publishers, 521 Fifth Avenue, New York, N.Y. 10017. Published simultaneously in Canada by Fitzhenry & Whiteside Limited, Toronto.

FIRST EDITION

Designer: Janice Stern

Library of Congress Cataloging in Publication Data

Bumagin, Victoria E
  Aging is a family affair.

  Bibliography: p.
  Includes index.
  1. Old age. 2. Aged—Family relationships.
3. Aging. I. Hirn, Kathryn F., joint author. II. Title.
HQ1061.B84 1979   301.43'5   78-22459
ISBN 0-690-01823-1

79 80 81 82 83 10 9 8 7 6 5 4 3 2 1

Contents

"To See Ourselves as Others See Us." The Overloaded Fuse: Dealing with Demands. Acknowledgment Versus Action. When Action Is Requested, Then Refused. Setting Limits Versus Withdrawal. How to Say No Without Feeling Guilty. The Protectiveness Trap and How to Get Out of It. The Mirage of Perfection. The Effective Use of Anger. Old Dogs Can Learn New Tricks. Creating Second Chances: Finding Sources of Help. Peer Groups as Facilitators. The Advantages of Different Perspectives

Preface
Should We Worry?

Mother, age seventy-eight, has fallen on the ice while on a shopping trip. She didn't break anything, but is painfully bruised. It is difficult for her to move about, even in the house. Should she continue to live alone?

Dad, age eighty-three, had an appointment with his dentist yesterday. He forgot to go. He says he thought it was Tuesday instead of Friday. Is he becoming senile?

As our parents or grandparents approach the seventies and eighties, we worry about such questions, as do our aging relatives themselves. There is cause for concern: the over-sixty-five population is estimated at 23,500,000 and is expected to reach 30,000,000 by the year 2000. Since more people are living longer and the incidence of chronic illness increases with age, medical expenses can be astronomical. The children of the elderly may be approaching retirement and may, at the same time, still be supporting college-age children of their own. Where do their responsibilities lie? And how will they find time and energy to lead their own lives when from both directions they are beset by demands, subtle or outspoken, for emotional or financial support?

Because of the rapidity of social and technological changes in the recent past, the experience of aging in the twentieth century is a new one both for the elderly and for their families, but little has been written to describe the uniqueness of this stage of the life cycle for both generations.

In some ways, the families of the aged are in a situation similar to that of the parents of adolescents; like the elderly, adolescents are another high-risk population coping with an onslaught of physical, emotional, and social changes. But there is one difference: no matter how variously they experienced it, the parents of adolescents have been teenagers themselves. The families of the aged do not have this advantage. The experience is still ahead of them. Thus, even more than when they wrestle with understanding their teenagers, they may need help, reassurance about the process of aging, and a basic sense of what is normal, what is pathological, and what to do about it.

If the parents of children nearing their teens confined themselves to reading the newspapers, they would probably be scared out of their wits. Drug addiction—unwed pregnancy—school dropouts—violence—is this what their young people are headed for? By the same token, the families of those classified as senior citizens may well be terrified by scare headlines about nursing homes or statistics on senility. They may have a general impression that after sixty it's downhill all the way, that physical and mental deterioration are inevitable, and that institutionalization, probably in some third-rate nursing home, is the only available solution. Unless they have the good fortune to know a large number of healthy and successful old people, they may have no way of discovering that "it ain't necessarily so."

This book is intended to do three things. First, it is a guide to the varieties of behavior encountered in the years between sixty and ninety plus—a period of over thirty years and equivalent to half the life span we expected a generation ago. Old people probably exhibit more differences from each other in that thirty-plus year span than can be observed in any other age group. And why not? There is likely to be more of a range in years among the elderly themselves than there is between them and their children, and the old have had more time to grow and develop their own individuality.

Second, this is a book on coping, on alternatives for dealing with problems, and on bridging the communications gap that frequently exists between the generations and makes solutions more than difficult to achieve. It provides information on what situations should be cause for real concern, and how to get help. It deals with the anticipation of death, with bereavement and its aftermath, and with the new growth that can occur as the loss is worked through.

Third, the book is meant to provide reassurance, and a measure of comfort, for those times when we have done everything we could think of and the problem still didn't go away.

We have used a great many examples from our experience as geriatric social workers and as family members. Identifying details have, of course, been disguised and many of the persons and situations described are composites of several. These stories are not, and do not pretend to be, a comprehensive listing of possible circumstances or reactions. That would require not a volume but an encyclopedia. Rather, they are intended to provide more vivid illustrations than can be achieved by description alone and to suggest parallels or contrasts in the reader's experience. They also constitute a tribute to those who have taught us the most about what it means to be old—the aged and their families. We hope that their stories will bring to you, as they have to us, a reassurance that old age, like all the other ages, can be a time of growing, challenge, and discovery.

The development of this book also owes a great deal to the elders in our own families, particularly Joachim and Maria Ginzberg and Genevieve Fitch, who have given us delightful role models of aging. For assistance in the actual writing we are greatly indebted to Esther Goldman of the Council for Jewish Elderly and to Elaine Switzer of the University of Chicago, who read and criticized the manuscript. Louisa O. Hellegers provided valuable editorial help. Finally, we owe a very special thanks to Victor I. Bumagin for his love, encouragement, criticism, and continuous support of our venture.

V. E. B.
K. F. H.

1

Social Changes: Losses and Gains

Two women sat at opposite ends of the interviewing room of a busy social service agency, each on the edge of her chair. One was probably in her mid-fifties, although she could have passed for a young forty—slender, smartly dressed, competent-looking. She had been crying. The other was tiny, birdlike, her gray hair pulled back in a tight bun. She perched grimly on a straight chair, her hands clasped tightly together, her black eyes snapping. She evoked the image of a pioneer mother, ready to defend her homestead. Perhaps she had a premonition.

As the social worker approached them, the younger woman introduced herself as Mrs. Harris and the other woman, her mother, as Mrs. Mecklenberg. Then she burst out, "You've got to convince my mother to move into a home for the aged. We can't go on like this!" Mrs. Mecklenberg glared. "I've told you over and over I'll do no such thing." She turned to the social worker. "Don't listen to her. I knew I shouldn't have come."

Mrs. Harris cut in. "Mother, you're being unreasonable." She leaned toward the social worker confidentially, and almost whispered, "You know, it's not safe—she fell—she's all alone. . . ."

Mrs. Mecklenberg heard her.

"So what if I did fall?" she retorted. "I suppose *you* never tripped? Is anybody asking *you* to move?"

"But, Mother, you're eighty years old!"

The social worker finally got a word in edgewise. "Where are you living, Mrs. Mecklenberg?"

Mrs. Harris answered for her. "In Michigan City—and it's just awful now. Terrible neighborhood . . ."

"You expect me to run away from a bunch of ruffians? Your father and I *built* that house."

Bit by bit the story came out. Mrs. Mecklenberg was living alone in the house she had shared with her husband for forty years. Mrs. Harris, her only daughter, lived too far away for frequent visits. Last winter, Mrs. Mecklenberg's furnace broke down. She had no heat for a week, and could not find a repairman. By the time her daughter was able to arrange for one, Mrs. Mecklenberg had developed a severe bronchial infection and was alone and bedridden for a long time. Then, a few weeks ago, she came down with the flu. There was no one to nurse her at home, so she stayed with Mrs. Harris during her convalescence—an experience neither of them enjoyed. Mrs. Mecklenberg went home two weeks ago, but calls Mrs. Harris every day "to complain": she's not feeling too well—another neighbor moved—the children next door are too noisy—the butcher forgot to deliver yesterday—she's not feeling so well. . . .

"I know she's not feeling well," Mrs. Harris summarized. "But she's so stubborn—she won't go anywhere except to our house—and I *know* that she wants to come and live with me—but I just *can't.* . . . I'm sorry, Mother."

"Live with you, indeed!" Mrs. Mecklenberg sniffed. "Better I should be in my grave."

"But, Mother . . ."

"Don't 'but Mother' me! I've been managing for eighty years, haven't I?"

She turned to the interviewer. "Every day I shop—I cook—I clean my house—I work in my garden—you should see my petunias—Mrs. Johnson can't get over them."

Now it was Mrs. Harris's turn. "But her heart isn't what it used to be, and her asthma is getting worse," she protested.

"So—just because I wheeze a little she wants to take my home away." Mrs. Mecklenberg also addressed the social worker. "I tell her the news and she thinks the world is coming to an end."

"It sounds like you're doing very well," the social worker ventured.

Mrs. Mecklenberg agreed vehemently. She described her daily activities in great detail once again, and then began to talk about her town and the many committees on which she was serving. She recalled earlier days when she and her husband considered themselves leaders of the community, and related how now she was always invited and escorted to all town events. She went on and on.

"You're trying so hard to be convincing, Mrs. Mecklenberg," the interviewer said, finally. "You're trying so hard you don't seem to notice that I agree with you. It's wonderful that you are so active. Still, it's not as easy as it used to be, is it?"

"Well, what do you expect? I'm eighty years old, after all!"

The social worker turned to Mrs. Harris before the daughter could pounce on this admission. "It *is* pretty scary when we see our parents beginning to slow down. It's clear that you are worried. But perhaps it isn't time to make any changes yet. Your mother seems to be managing very well."

Instead of an onslaught of protest, Mrs. Harris first looked bewildered, then relieved. "You mean"—for the first time she faced Mrs. Mecklenberg with a question instead of an answer—"you mean you really don't want to move in with me?"

"Isn't that what I've been telling you?" snapped the old lady. But her hands were no longer gripping the sides of her chair.

They talked a few minutes longer with the social worker, about practicalities: transportation, doctors, ways of getting extra help in the house, assurance that consultative help would be available "if and when" some other need should arise.

When the ladies rose to leave, Mrs. Mecklenberg risked her first real smile. "You really must come and see my petunias," she said.

Two days later, a note arrived from Mrs. Harris. "You have helped me so much," she wrote.

How had the social worker helped, after all? What had she done but call the attention of each to what the other was saying? Nothing had really changed. The situation that had felt so desperate before they came in was still exactly the same. Mrs. Mecklenberg would continue to live, somewhat precariously, in her house in Michigan City, tending her petunias and complaining. Mrs. Harris would continue to worry about her, and to meditate on "if and when." So what was different? Nothing—except that, perhaps, they had begun to listen to each other.

The Communication Gap

Why is it so hard for adults and their parents to listen to each other? The daily preoccupation of many old people and their children is the fact that all of them are facing a set of tasks for which society has provided virtually no preparation. There is no dearth of books and experts to tell us what to expect in all the phases of child development, from the first tooth to the first date. The tasks of childhood, adolescence, and young adulthood have been very fully described. From a variety of sources we can absorb conventional and unconventional wisdom about career preparation, about the changing face of marriage, about "identity." But what happens after the children leave home, when the career winds down, when the increasing feebleness of a parent brings us up against the fact of death, and the assessment of the meaning of our lives? What happens in the years between forty and seventy—or eighty—or ninety? Compared to the detailed road maps of the first half of life, existing guidelines for the second half look like the Empty Quarter of Saudi Arabia—uncharted territory.

The final decades of life are usually marked by physical, social, and emotional losses and changes. Some of these are major and obviously all-encompassing, such as widowhood. Others, like changing values, the departure of old friends, or the gradual decline of energy, are more insidious. Also, not only losses but gains may characterize these years; there might be grandchildren, second careers, different styles of leisure, new friends, even new spouses. Those who have developed their individuality and coping abilities over a life span of sixty or seventy or eighty years exhibit a wide range of personal styles in dealing with all these changes— from becoming more dependent on their children to becoming more active politically. This bewildering variety may make it very difficult for the several generations to communicate about what is happening. The task is further complicated by the fact that these changes have not been previously experienced either by the old people or by their younger relatives; that they are often unanticipated; and that they may seem too painful to address head-on, especially when several events occur at once. For those affected, a way of protecting themselves may be to deny that anything is different, at least until the new and strange situation feels less threatening or less overwhelming. In the meantime, intergenerational communications may suffer.

Change Is Always Surprising

Children become teenagers; Mom becomes liberated; Grandpa becomes old. The most consistent feature of human experience is change. In spite of this consistency, we are usually surprised by change. The infant takes his first step; the child goes off to school; the adolescent's voice deepens; the pigtailed tomboy becomes a bride; and we are astonished.

Likewise, when Father retires, when Mother's step is slower than it used to be and her hair is "suddenly" gray, when Grandma has a major illness, we experience the sense of being caught unprepared.

Even the changes that can be anticipated do not always happen in the expected order. Sometimes the younger or healthier people, to whom the aged looked for support, are themselves the victims of illness or misfortune. When this happens, the old people may feel bereft and cheated. Children are not supposed to die; healthy breadwinners are not supposed to become disabled. But sometimes they do. When it happens, the rest of the family have to cope with the resulting practical dislocations as well as with their own sense of injustice and outrage. It may be some consolation to such families to realize that their situation is not as unique as they suppose.

Not only do family changes, expected or unexpected, occur, but social and technological changes are happening with a quickness reminiscent of early assembly-line speedups or silent-movie sequences of the Keystone Kops. Covered wagons and jet planes are spanned by the memory of one generation.

For this generation and their families, it is necessary to erect some landmarks in the wilderness, and begin to develop a map that will help other travelers to know where they are. Not only must the changing circumstances of the later years be clarified, but also the developments and changes in self-image, self-esteem, and the appreciation of the value of one's life.

And most of all, the traumatic events and the social changes that affect the lives of older people must be viewed not as catastrophes but as benchmarks in the continuum of human life, to be experienced, endured, and then coped with as ingeniously as energy, will, and habitual patterns of dealing with problems will allow. Those who live into their seventies and eighties and nineties have already learned, over a long life span, to deal with crises. All they need to realize now, and all their families might need to be reminded of, is that the process is still the same, only coming at a later time.

What actually is involved in the social changes that confront old people? The following pages describe some of the most common changes as well as a sample of the ways in which people deal with them. The list is not encyclopedic, and does not pretend to include every possible situation or response. Rather, it illustrates some of the infinite variety of human coping styles, and the growth that can result from them.

Changing Values

As they get older, the aged watch the world around them changing, and with it the erosion of values with which they grew up and which they held dear. Contemplating the changes to which they are subjected may sometimes make them feel like strangers in their own country. Like immigrants, who have left language and family and familiar landmarks behind and struggle with the transition from one culture to another, they try to "sing the Lord's song in a strange land." Their exasperation and puzzlement are understandable. Crossing an ocean of water or crossing an ocean of time may not be so different. For instance, Grandpa, whether born in Europe or in an earlier America, expected his handiwork to endure, and was mindful of waste. Now his children belong to a "throwaway" generation; they have no room to keep mementos.

Mr. Lande's basement storeroom is full of old furniture, electrical fittings, a motor salvaged from a discarded washing machine, the cabinet from an extinct radio-phonograph, a burnt-out television set. His son is impatient with the apparent chaos. "Get rid of it, Dad. You'll never use it, and it's a fire hazard. Even if you did have a use for something, you'd never find it in here." "Nonsense," retorts the elder Lande. "I know exactly where everything is. You young people are wasteful—don't know how to prepare for a rainy day. When the next Depression comes, you'll see I was right."

With current increased concern about economy, recycling, and a return to nature, Mr. Lande's attitude may strike a more responsive chord in his grandchildren than in his children, and it may be of some comfort to him that history and approaches to life have a way of repeating themselves.

Loss of Contemporaries

Living in "the brave new world," Grandfather and Grandmother have had the company of those who remember the world as it used to be. But with advancing age, more and more of these disappear, and with their departure, who is left to share the memories? With loss of their contemporaries, their vision shrinks. Who will remember the taste of wild raspberries along the pasture fence, or what Aunt Nettie said when the cat tipped over the churn, now that brother John is gone?

Not all departures are caused by death. It may only seem like that. Friends and children may move to other states or other neighborhoods. Sometimes a whole community empties almost overnight, leaving the few stragglers surrounded by strangers and deprived of familiar landmarks.

Mrs. Cohen, a vigorous lady in her eighties, applied for admission to a retirement home. She had been living in a changing neighborhood and was asked if she had trouble with her new neighbors, most of whom were black or Puerto Rican. "Oh, no," she said, shrugging, "no trouble at all. But my friends were gone, my son was gone, the *shul* and the rabbi were gone—what was to stay for?"

One of her black contemporaries experienced the same problem in reverse. A new resident of Mrs. Cohen's neighborhood, Mrs. Cooper regularly made an hour's trip on public transportation to return to her old church. Asked if she did not feel welcome in the churches in her new community, she said that wasn't it. She tried to describe what was lacking: "A white preacher can use the same text, preach the same sermon as the black preacher—but it's got no taste—nothing to chew on—no . . . well, no *heart.*"

In addition to the effects of changing neighborhoods on those who remain, the fact of the change is likely to stir up panic in family members who live elsewhere. Children may exert pressure to move because "Mother mustn't stay in that terrible place." If the pressure is successful, Mother may be precipitously transferred to a suburban house where no one is home all day and transportation does not exist, or to an unneeded institution. Under the whip of fear, all the implications of a move may not be considered, and the end result may be more isolation instead of less.

Changing Relationships

Along with the loss of the old—friends, neighborhoods, landmarks—comes the arrival of the new. Those who retain energy and enthusiasm to invest in others may find the changes ultimately rewarding: the new children next door who love homemade cookies or the neighbor down the hall who shares a chess hobby will foster new relationships; the gregarious couple who spend much of their retirement in travel will continue to gain new friends at every step and can perpetuate their new contacts in their worldwide corre- spondence. One lady who recently celebrated her ninetieth birthday received more than a hundred cards, over half of them from people she met after she was sixty-five. Those who have a knack for friendship are not likely to lose it in old age.

Not only losses, but shifts in daily lives, can affect the balance in relationships of long standing. For instance, marriages that have lasted for many years may be subjected to new stresses when one spouse becomes seriously ill, or when retirement forces a couple to spend much more time together than they have been accustomed to. Until they learn, as Kahlil Gibran wrote in *The Prophet,* to find "spaces in their togetherness" and to devise ways of meeting their separate needs, the new demands may be overwhelming. A wife who is caring for a severely disabled husband can be torn between resentment at the demands placed on her and guilt over her resentment. Exhausted though she may be, she may resist not only institutional care but even any temporary relief, such as a part-time housekeeper or companion. The care she insists on giving may be meticulous but hostile. If the invalid retaliates by noncooperation— through incontinence, for instance—the vicious circle of resentment-guilt-hostility-retaliation may be intensified to the point where both parties are locked in a bitter but silent battle. "See how much I do for him!" the caretaker cries, while the one who needs care defiantly says "No!" by silent bodily actions. Such couples often remind observers of an angry mother and a resistant two-year-old. If the caretaker can be helped to recognize and accept his or her own needs, the pressure is decreased and the invalid may turn out to be far less helpless than he or she appeared to be.

The rest of the family may be able to provide help once they realize the plight of the caretaker. The first step is recognizing that exhaustion and frustration are not the natural order of things but problems that need to be solved. A part-time companion or assistant, perhaps a college student or a mother of school-age children who wants to work a few hours a week, may provide the necessary time for refreshment and reconstitution. Day-care programs, now becoming available in some areas, may be a source of stimulation and increased independence for the disabled person as well as a means of relief for the family. The prerequisite for using such services is the realization that martyrdom is neither necessary nor helpful.

Adjustment to a spouse's disability is difficult enough when the one who must assume the caretaker role has always been the dominant member of the marriage. But sometimes the reverse happens. Mrs. London, for instance, had always been a volatile and rather petulant person, subject to mood swings and temper tantrums. Mr. London had been the stable one. Calm and practical, he provided a buffer between the children and their mother's outbursts while they were growing up. When, later, Mrs. London developed diabetes, he watched over her diet and curbed her tendency to self-indulgent food binges. However, in his early seventies, Mr. London began to suffer from blackouts and lapses of memory. Mrs. London was frantic. She raged at him in a futile effort to make him "like he was before." She could not tolerate losing her caretaker, or learn to become one herself. Mr. London eventually took refuge with one of his children, which, of course, affected the life of the younger family. When an existing equilibrium is upset by a major change in circumstances, all hell can break loose until a new one is established. In such circumstances, the family may need to seek professional help to understand the new situation and its effect and to contemplate and work on a solution.

Illness is not the only cause of shifts in balance. Retirement can create a very different life pattern. The wife who has been at home all along may find her suddenly retired husband "underfoot" all day. If he is irritable and at loose ends, she may be at a loss to know what to do with him and may resent having the even tenor of her ways disturbed. As one wife put it, "I took him for better or for worse. But for lunch?"

In a household where the working wife continues in her job after the husband's retirement, she may expect him to cope with unaccustomed household responsibilities. The reversal of their roles may be difficult for both of them. This situation is, in many ways, similar to that of the younger family in which one spouse is unemployed. Either way, when the structure of life is altered in a family, relationships are also subject to examination and change. A new balance may be created (or the old balance recaptured) when the unemployed spouse finds a job and the retired person develops a hobby, a second career, or some other way of structuring daily life. In the newness of such a situation, a couple may learn to do together what they have never done or have done separately before, or they may rejoice in and respect the individuality of independent pursuits.

With aging, marital relationships are affected in other ways as well. Sometimes a marriage that has existed uncomfortably for years is terminated when a couple, aware that time is limited, take stock of their life satisfactions. The soaring divorce rate affects old people as well as young ones. The divorce of a child may push parents toward examining their own relationship. They may decide that "enough is enough," or they may look for ways to improve the situation. Older couples are beginning to make their appearance in the offices of marriage counselors and, where the motivation for change is strong enough, they can reap the same benefits available to younger couples. In fact, the older couple's willingness to change may be increased by their recognition that time is short and must be used or lost forever.

Reordering Priorities

Consciousness of the limitation of time often leads to establishing priorities and allocating time and interest to things that matter most. In a way, this means relinquishing some old patterns and choosing new ways of distributing one's energy. A man nearing sixty stated that after he and his wife moved to a new community, they did not expend as much effort seeking new acquaintances as they had when they were younger, because "we're more particular now." What mattered for them were the ties with children and grandchildren, and the leisurely development of those friendships that were really congenial.

Setting priorities means attending to one's own felt needs rather than to social or family expectations, or even to one's previous self-expectation. Priorities shift over time, and the ability to review and change them is a sign of growth.

Widowhood

Old friends die or move away; neighborhoods change; children grow up and leave home; spouses come to a final parting. The empty-nest reaction of the middle-aged mother becomes the empty-hearth mourning of the elderly widow. When the marriage has been a close and sympathetic one, the surviving partner may feel like half a person, as if part of one's very self had died. Yet, paradoxically, a good marriage appears to be easier to survive than a disappointing one. However intense the grief, the one left behind eventually picks up the threads of life and weaves a new pattern.

Will and Marcia Freeson had been married more than fifty years. They raised four children and numerous foster children, and, in their later years, welcomed a dozen grand-children. Theirs was a home that people liked to visit and to linger in, for, despite many problems, its inhabitants had so much fun together. Anyone who talked with Will or Marcia soon realized how lucky each felt about having the other for a partner.

Not long after their fiftieth anniversary, Will died of lung cancer. Marcia, of course, missed him acutely. Yet she maintained her other relationships, and flung herself into continuing a project that Will had started. A year or two after his death, she began taking long trips with her sister-in-law, who was also recently widowed. Her bubbling enthusiasm for life revived. Even without Will, she was still a person.

By contrast, Evelyn and Frank Barnes spent twenty years bickering. They expressed their regrets at having married each other loudly and frequently. Yet when Frank died, Evelyn was not relieved. She spent months reciting her grievances against Frank—what a terrible husband he had been, how badly off he had left her, how frightened she had been when he fell and she had to get him to the hospital, what poor care he had received, how indifferent all her friends and relatives were. She debated endlessly whether to move or not to move, and could not get any plan under way. Without Frank to fight with, she could not seem to exist. Even the marriage whose chief justification is to provide a battleground is difficult to relinquish.

Then, too, there are those marriages where the conflicts are not out in the open. Here, one spouse has been almost totally subservient to the needs of the other. The survivors of these often seem shadowlike, without lives of their own. The old-fashioned term for widow ("relict") truly applies to them. Sometimes, however, observers are surprised by the sudden independence and competence developed by the former "professional wife." The prognosis seems to depend on the survivor's achievement of independent personhood (past or potential), as well as on the quality of the marriage.

The loss of a life partner means not only the loss of a friend and peer, not only the end of a relationship, but a change of status that affects every aspect of one's life.

When Mrs. Belofsky became so ill that she had to enter a nursing home, her husband spent every afternoon with her. She was incontinent and frequently confused and sometimes she did not even recognize him. To outsiders, the visits appeared a thankless burden, but when she died, Mr. Belofsky felt that his purpose in life had disappeared. How would he structure his day without his wife to visit and care for? How would he develop a new life style at eighty-five?

Emotional needs do not decrease with loss, any more than financial needs lessen with reduced income. The problem is to find new supports to replace the missing one. Those who have lost a spouse, for instance, may seek closer connections with their children, their remaining brothers and sisters, or their religious organizations. For a while, it may seem to the bereaved one that friends and family, particularly children, are less attentive than they used to be. The children may, in fact, be devoting more time and attention to the parent who is bereft, but it seems like less because the need is greater.

Developing Alternative Supports

Whether there has been loss of productivity by retirement or loss by death, there needs to be a period of mourning—

a necessary pause in the pattern of day-to-day life. When restitution begins to occur, as it will, many who have lost spouses begin to seek new contacts or interests. In addition to, or instead of, tightening family and friendship ties, some people are able to find friends and achievement through volunteer activities. There is often a demand for teachers' helpers, foster grandparents, or visitors to nursing homes, to orphanages, or to isolated people in their own homes, as well as for various special skills. One retired engineer has developed a volunteer repair service for elderly people who are financially and physically unable to obtain such services commercially.

Perhaps the chief obstacle to the use of old people for such tasks is the lack of expectation by society that they have anything to contribute. All too often, older citizens are seen as having problems but not as being part of any solutions. It is a curious commentary on our views and priorities that we tell our most experienced citizens to turn to leisure but rely on the younger, less experienced citizens to control the economy and conduct the business affairs of the country. It reminds one of the boy who was asked, in an examination, what George Washington would think of the United Nations if he were still living. The youngster replied, "If he were alive today, he would be so extremely old that his opinions on any subject would be worthless." The assumption that not much can be expected of the elderly makes it more difficult for the elderly to expect very much of themselves.

The Gray Panther Approach: An Alternative to Depression

The issues of power, subjection, and self-image have been very much in the public eye for the past few years as various groups have advocated for their own needs and their place in the sun of prosperity and prestige. Increasing numbers of elderly people have begun to see their problems as the result of powerlessness, and to push for more control of their lives.The Gray Panthers is an organization of people who oppose discrimination based on "ageism," and who lobby for more adequate services for the elderly. Their approach is useful not only because it increases public awareness of the need for such services, but also because it helps to increase the self-esteem of older citizens. Being able to see one's plight as the result of society's failures rather than one's own inadequacies can be very liberating. Those who feel that they deserve a better reward for a lifetime of contribution are both more likely to get it and better able to tolerate being without it for the time being. Taking action is an excellent means of alleviating anxiety and combating hopelessness, especially when the action results in some kind of improvement. Even when no improvement is immediately apparent, being able to act is a powerful reminder that one is not a pawn. Further, the recognition that society is responsible for the inequities in the current status of old people is likely to result in anger and in active efforts to effect change, and this will dissipate feelings of self-blame, depression, and apathy. "Do not go gentle into that good night," counsels Dylan Thomas. This is also the view of the Gray Panthers, who advocate an open approach to all issues in aging—from facing indignity to facing death. (The Gray Panthers, as well as other sources of help and self-help, are listed in Appendix II.)

When Personal Choices Conflict with Family Expectations

Developing one's own emotional support system in the face of changing needs is one of the necessities of coping with the job of growing older. However, the life styles adopted by old people do not always fit social and family expectations. Grandma may prefer to play cards than to baby-sit for the family, or she may scandalize her children by winning a prize for ballroom dancing, perhaps as the partner of a married man. Grandpa, a recent widower, may take off on a cruise and come back with a woman half his age. His brother may join the ranks of those who boycott grapes or picket the White House. The reaction of family and associates is likely to be "Really! At their age!", to which a proper reply might be, "Really! Why not?"

The Myths of Aged Sexuality

Of all the options that may be selected by older people, sexual interests are most likely to arouse strong opposition from family or society. Older people have to contend both with their own anxieties and with the cultural assumption that romantic interests and sexual behavior for them are "probably impossible, possibly immoral and unquestionably absurd."[1]

A British television play entitled *Love Story* described a romance which blossomed in a residential establishment for the elderly. In a scene where the couple decide to share a bed, great care was taken to establish that companionship was their only objective. The producers apparently assumed, perhaps rightly, that their audience would not have found a sexual motivation acceptable. In this age of sexual explicitness, why is it that we have a hard time seeing such a relationship as plausible, when love affairs among younger unmarrieds are commonplace? Could we have been shocked into reality if the portrayal of these two people in their seventies had carried us into their marriage and then to the nuptial bed?

American culture stresses youthful beauty and athletic sexual performance so heavily that men in their thirties begin to worry about impotence as they recall their teen years. Women are bombarded with recipes for remaining youthful—hair dyes, wrinkle creams, and all manner of gimmicks which promise to preserve the image of the eighteen-year-old girl. The clear message is that only the young are beautiful, and only the beautiful can deserve or enjoy sex. The advantages of maturity, the increased richness of personality and capacity for emotional involvement are ignored by Madison Avenue. The fears of sexual inadequacy that plague Americans of all ages are thus intensified by fears of aging and loss of function.

Another source of anxiety to would-be lovers is health: for example, heart patients might assume that they have to give up sex to avoid endangering their lives. This is usually not the case, but many are too shy to ask the doctor about this or other conditions which may make sex difficult or uncomfortable. It is unfortunate that many doctors, like the rest of society, take an attitude of "At your age, what does it matter?"

It is encouraging that this attitude is no longer as prevalent as it used to be. Ten years ago there was virtually no attention paid to sexual needs and problems among old people. Since then, a number of research studies have demonstrated that men and women do continue to have active sex lives in their eighties, nineties, and beyond, if they are reasonably healthy and have an available partner. (The older generation could have told us so long ago, had we thought to ask!) Professional literature on the subject is beginning to take this into account, including a handbook for older lovers, *Sex After Sixty,* by Robert Butler and Myrna Lewis, which deals practically and sympathetically with many of the physical and emotional aspects of aging sexuality.

Sex in the Nursing Home

One setting in which very little recognition has thus far been given to sexual needs is that of nursing homes and other protected residences for the elderly. This is probably one reason why many old people see institutionalization as equivalent to the loss of adulthood.

Few nursing homes or homes for the aged make provisions for couples (married or otherwise) to be alone together. An eighty-four-year-old in such a facility who asks permission to share his girlfriend's room is likely to be laughed at or greeted with horror. One director of a retirement home once stated that she discourages any consideration of marriage among the residents. She explains to them that while the courtship stage focuses everyone's attention on the lovers, the bloom soon falls off the bush. The couple will find that their marriage requires a lot of adjustments and they will undoubtedly begin to fight—so who needs it? One wonders if she would give the same advice to younger lovers, even though their destiny may be the same.

Other opportunities for sexual expression are also not easily available. The passes that elderly residents make at young nurses, or the flirtatious manner many an older man adopts with a young female helper, are likely to be seen as evidence of psychiatric aberration. Coming from a young man, the same behavior would be laughed off. Likewise, we are becoming more lenient about masturbation among the young, but can we tolerate, condone—perhaps even encourage—masturbation as a sexual outlet for the old?

Despite the restrictions of institutional settings, a few

hardy souls do manage to beat the system. An eighty-two-year-old resident of a home for the aged, who had been a "madam" in Europe, was reputed to have kept the male residents very happy until a stroke put her out of commission. Nevertheless, she found a way of retrieving some of the loss: she persuaded her doctor to include in her physical-therapy order the instructions that she was to have "vaginal massage" at least once a day!

Remarriage and Other Outrages

The myths of aged sexuality make second marriages more difficult to achieve. If Dad decides to remarry at seventy-seven, for instance, he may stir up an unexpected hornets' nest of family reactions. "Poor man—he's so lonely" may suddenly become "He must be crazy!" Why it should be crazy to want a companion and a sexual partner at eighty but not at fifty or thirty or twenty is a question seldom raised. Martin A. Berezin, a psychiatrist, has noted the evidence of cultural prejudice in the assumption that "what is considered to be virility at 25 becomes lechery at 65."[2] It may also be considered evidence of senility—a far more cruel stereotype; given a choice of epithets, most of us would rather be labeled as sinners than as fools! The cultural blindness to sexuality in the old is compounded by the tendency of children of all ages to disbelieve that *their* parents could have sexual needs or interests. The man or woman of fifty can have just as hard a time with the acceptance of such an idea as does the child of five or the adolescent of fifteen. And while nonmarital sexual interests may be ignored, an actual marriage in the family cannot be.

When David Galt began dating Libby Franklin, his family was at first delighted. Mr. Galt had been living with his daughter Martha since his wife's death, and had been finding the time hanging heavy on his hands. Martha and her family thought it was nice for Dad to have a new interest in life, and he and Libby were "so cute" together. When they started to plan a June wedding, however, the climate suddenly changed. Libby became "that woman" who was out to "get Dad's money." David's tendency to forget appointments and lose keys was seen as evidence of incompetence, and when he changed his will so as to settle part of his estate on his intended bride, his daughter was convinced that he was no longer of sound mind. As the wedding date approached, Martha took to her bed with a sick headache. She could not bring herself to attend the ceremony, so while Libby's children and grandchildren turned out in force, the groom's side of the chapel was empty. David was deeply hurt, and a permanent estrangement from his daughter resulted.

It is amazing how similar the reactions of children to a parent's remarriage can be to those of parents considering the marriage of a son or daughter: "He isn't good enough for her." "She's such a scatterbrain—she'll never make a proper home for him." "We never see them anymore—they spend the holidays with *her* family." It is so hard to let go, and to accord each other adult status.

Nonetheless, marriage among the after-sixty set has somewhat different tasks and hazards from marriage among the young. Family reactions are likely, even if they are not as severe as those of David Galt's daughter, and physical and financial deficits are more prevalent with advancing years. In addition, when a young pair marries, their families usually accept that they will grow and develop together. For the older couple, it is assumed that they are what they are, and that change and adjustment would be less likely to occur. When the older people themselves begin to believe this, or when the prospect of change becomes too hard to contemplate, the result is a denial of sexual needs as well as the lack of a partner.

To Wed or Not to Wed

Even those who accept their emotional and sexual needs openly and honestly and are fortunate enough to find potential partners have a dilemma: marriage may create a host of financial and family complications which are perhaps more easily addressed by cohabitation than by legal union. For those who dare to become such "sinners," acceptance of their life style is more likely to come from their grandchildren than from their children, with inherent risk to the parent-child relationships in both family units.

Middle-aged adults have hardly recovered from the shock of seeing their children choosing partners without benefit of clergy when they discover their aged parents doing likewise. "The children are living together, and now, for goodness' sakes, so are our parents. Is nothing sacred?" Members of the middle generation are generally apt to be the ones most vulnerable to questions and second thoughts about their marriages, careers, and life accomplishments. To see the values they have upheld, and which they learned from their parents, apparently abandoned by those same parents may feel like betrayal indeed. Or is it, perhaps, permission to re-examine and consider change—a reminder that if seventy-year-olds can alter the habits of a lifetime, fifty may not be too late?

Perhaps the situation was best put in perspective by an eighty-one-year-old woman who was living with a gentleman of eighty-four. Some of her neighbors complained to her son about his mother's morals. When he visited her to discuss the situation, she reassured him: "Now, dear, don't worry. We're both old enough to know what we're doing—and I'm on the Pill—so what can happen?"

Not only financial and family repercussions, but the prospect or actuality of failing health may result in reluctance to marry. If the marriage does take place, health factors may soon trigger feelings of disappointment. The parties to a new marriage may not be as committed to taking care of each other "in sickness and in health" as the veterans of twenty, thirty, or fifty years together often are. When one partner in a new alliance does become ill or disabled, a new balance—or imbalance—is created between the partners and their previously existing families.

When Horace Grant, seventy-three, met and courted Millie Hayes, sixty-nine, both were vigorous people who loved to travel. Their respective families were delighted with the new alliance, and all went well until Horace suffered a stroke. At that point, Millie's children urged her to bow out. "Look, Mom, you nursed Dad for six years. Wasn't that enough? Horace has a daughter, after all. Let her take care of him. You've only been married two years, for heaven's sake!" Horace's daughter, for her part, was more than ready to assume responsibility for his care. She moved him halfway across the country so that he could enter a rehabilitation hospital in the city where she lived. Her plan was to move him from the hospital to a nearby retirement home, where she could keep an eye on him.

The forgotten factors in this equation were Horace and Millie, who were not so ready to give up their new life together. When Horace entered the hospital, Millie insisted on going along. She moved in with Horace's daughter and used her home as a base for her daily visits to the hospital.

The daughter found her presence burdensome, and thought she was impeding Horace's progress by "waiting on him hand and foot." Horace, however, was making a recovery unanticipated by his doctors. He was determined to learn to walk again so that he could rejoin Millie in their home. Her presence and continued interest in the marriage provided him with the best of incentives for getting well. Eventually he succeeded, and the couple did resume their life together. They moved a little more slowly, and both sets of children worried about them. Horace and Millie probably worried, too, but they were determined not to relinquish the time that was still available to them.

Not all couples are as strong-willed, or as lucky, as Horace and Millie. Engaging in new relationships always involves risk, and for those beset by physical and financial deficits, the risks may be overwhelming. Some choose to avoid the dangers; others perfer to take their chances with the hazards of life, rather than waste their remaining time in loneliness. As in all other matters, the choice must be an individual one.

Grandchildren and Other Renewals

Whether or not they develop new peer relationships, many older people find their greatest satisfaction in their grandchildren or other young people.

Despite the inadequacies of the human condition, and against all advice to the contrary, the new generations continue to arrive. Grandparents often have a very special relationship with these newcomers. One grandson, now grown up, remembered when he was a kid and movies cost a nickel, and times were hard and money in very short supply; it was Grandma who somehow always found a nickel for him. Other grandchildren remember the wonders of Granddad's workshop, the smells of Grammy's kitchen. Grandparents and grandchildren often seem to have more success in understanding each other than the middle generation has with either the old or the young.

Perhaps it is because the parental "should"s do not intrude so much. A youngster can listen entranced to Grandmother's stories of her childhood without feeling any threat to his autonomy, while a parent's "when I was your age" pronouncements are apt to be received as a criticism. Meanwhile, the parent is likely to be more concerned about Grandmother's blood pressure than about her storytelling ability, more interested in Johnny's homework than in his discovery of the family's own history. Grandparents and grandchildren, however, can indulge in the luxury of enjoyment without responsibility. Yet, paradoxically, that very enjoyment may be a vehicle of learning for the young and of validation for the old.

The fact that Grandmother tells the same story over and over, a characteristic that often irritates younger adults, may be a source of delight to a child. It is the child, after all, who demands to hear "The Three Bears" told in exactly the same way every night at bedtime until his parents are ready to fly out the window from exasperation and weariness. How wonderful it would be if Grandmother could take over the storytelling task, fulfilling both the child's need and her own, and leaving the parents free for activities necessary to their own stage of life!

What luxury grandparents and grandchildren share in the simple enjoyment of each other as people! It has been said that youth is too valuable to waste on children; isn't the quality of grandparenthood so valuable as to be envied?

When Mr. Belofsky (see page 16) felt so lost after his

wife's death, he found great comfort in his relationship with his grandchildren. With the help of a housekeeper, he was able to entertain them on birthdays and holidays, and to feel once more like a host in his own house, rather than always being a guest in theirs. He was particularly gratified when he was able to help one grandson prepare for his Bar Mitzvah and found that the nostalgia this evoked in the boy's father stimulated his participation in the studies. The photograph of the three of them studying together occupies a place of honor on Mr. Belofsky's dresser. He had not, after all, lost his role and purpose in life, for he had passed on a valued tradition to the new generation and others yet to come.

Grandchildren need not be one's own. It is not the blood tie alone that makes for a meaningful renewal of life. Mr. Pratt, an elderly man who had no close relatives, moved in with a family as a boarder. He lived with them for eight years and struck up a friendship with their young son. The youngster loved listening to Mr. Pratt's reminiscences— stories of the places he had seen, of the many trades he had followed, of how the country had changed in his lifetime. When he died, the only tears at his funeral were shed by the twelve-year-old boy who had just lost his best friend and teacher.

When the boy grew up, he became a political geographer. Was his choice of career influenced by those remembered stories? Perhaps.

Many adults can remember an older person—a teacher, a favorite uncle, a neighbor—who had that kind of impact on their lives. Sometimes the young people were in particular need of the help of an adult outside the immediate family, sometimes the meeting was one of chance, but always the benefits accrued on both sides.

A seventy-nine-year-old grandmother, whose own grandchildren had grown up and moved to other parts of the country, continued her contact with children by teaching in a preschool educational program. Later, she "adopted" the children of a recently arrived immigrant family, teaching them English, offering old-country treats along with her tutoring, and, in many ways, giving them the benefits of her long years in America. She remembered having been a bewildered newcomer herself, and she gained much gratification from befriending the new children as she had once been befriended.

Thus the veterans of life convey their experience to those who come after—if they have the capacity to give and can find recipients. The recipients are not always children. Second careers, long-cherished projects, sometimes just the practice of reminiscence may also serve to summarize and validate a lifetime. But it always helps, when considering the changes that aging brings, to have someone to talk to, to have someone who wants to hear.

2

The Economics of Aging: "Money Is Honey"

The Obsolete Generation: Loss of Role

At sixty-four, Mr. Benson was a busy executive: responsible, harassed, admired. On his yes or no depended the shape of the business and the careers of other men.

At sixty-five, Mr. Benson retired. His company had a mandatory retirement policy. Decisions he used to make are now made by others. Sometimes they ask his opinion, but nobody has to pay attention to it. He is responsible only for walking the dog and buying the daily newspaper. His wife tries to think up errands and activities that will take him out of the house; otherwise, he tries to organize her work. Last week a friend commented, "The world is your oyster, Bob. You don't have to do a thing you don't want to." Mr. Benson's face turned purple. "You don't know what you're talking about! These days, I feel as if I don't even cast a shadow."

In modern society, work opportunities decrease sharply long before sixty-five. Even forty-five-year-olds are considered "older workers" in current federal programs. This despite the fact that the law has recently been changed to postpone mandatory retirement to age seventy (although still permitting workers to retire and collect full Social Security benefits at age sixty-five if they choose to do so). While the new law may be an attempt to deal with age discrimination in the job market, passage of the law alone cannot answer the problem of negative attitudes toward old people, or, for instance, the high cost of insurance which often dissuades even those employers who would be willing to hire older workers. Thus many men and women in their fifties, with highly developed skills and long histories of responsible job performance, are considered virtually unemployable. How much more unemployable are those who have passed the "magic marker" of sixty-five!

What happens when a productive life style is suddenly thrown into reverse gear?

Retirement generally means the loss of the role that has defined most of one's adult life. When a man is no longer "Mr. Bell, the plumber," or "Mr. Johnson, the engineer," who is he? Is he "Mr. Bell, who used to be a plumber," or is he still a plumber who is no longer working? Is an engineer always an engineer?

Of course, this is not a problem reserved only for men. For women who have had their lives devoted to home and family and those many women who have had lifelong careers outside the home, the problem is the same. Retirement from motherhood or cessation of a job at best requires a great deal of adjustment. But the end of a period of structured productivity is particularly difficult for those whose lives have held few other interests. Retired people who can turn to their gardens, begin to travel, or indulge an old passion for music or mystery stories may feel less like "unpeople" when their careers come to an end than those whose lives revolved around their work, and whose work gave them a sense of self-worth, status, and total satisfaction.

For those fortunate enough to have learned to use and value leisure earlier in life, finding enjoyable leisure-time activities may be an adequate solution. For them, the days may not be long enough to pursue all their interests. If health and financial resources allow them to address and develop those interests, their retirement may be golden indeed. However, limited resources are very real restrictions on retirement activities. Interesting ways of spending leisure time are apt to be expensive. Inexpensive leisure may not only leave one's dreams unfulfilled, but may make one feel demeaned and worthless in a society where status so often depends on being able to spend money freely. Loss of status, for whatever reason, is depressive in its effects.

Further, and regardless of available resources, there are many people for whom work has provided not only the structure for their daily lives, but the main source of their self-esteem. For them, play is no substitute: it is not an acceptable way for an adult to spend the bulk of his time. The loss of his productive role may result in profound depression.

Families who are unaware of this sense of loss are often puzzled by the post-retirement behavior of their elders. When a previously reasonable man or woman becomes irritable, depressed, unaccountably bossy, and impossible to please, children and friends worry. Is Dad becoming "senile" (that dreaded word!)? Should they try to do something for him, or is it better to withdraw and pretend not to notice? These well-meant efforts are apt to fail dismally when all Dad has really lost is his sense of usefulness.

Miss Winchell took her father to the doctor because he was behaving strangely. Every morning he got up at seven, dressed as if for work, bought a paper, and took the train downtown. Once there, he ate breakfast in a drugstore, then walked up one street and down another, seemingly with no destination. At noon, he stopped for lunch or fed the squirrels in the park, then resumed his ramblings. Miss Winchell was afraid he was exhausting himself, perhaps losing his memory. He never seemed able to give a full account of where he had been or why. The doctor, after a few minutes' conversation with Mr. Winchell, diagnosed his malady as post-retirement depression. It was not Mr. Winchell's arteries that were closing up, but his options.

Then a local community center offered Mr. Winchell a chance to use his carpentry skills doing volunteer repair work. He became a changed man. He not only kept the center's chairs mended and its doors unstuck, but he organized a group of teenagers to redo their recreation room, oversaw the paint job, and gave pointers in the technique of refinishing furniture. Both Mr. Winchell and the kids were delighted with the results, and with themselves. It was not only having something to do but feeling that the task was useful that allowed Mr. Winchell to feel like an adult again.

We are only beginning to tap the vast potential of the skills of retired people. One of the organizations that are seeking to use these skills is RSVP. (Retired Senior Volunteers Program. See Appendix IV for addresses.) Another, which provides a small stipend as well as a useful role, is Foster Grandparents. (See Appendix IV.) Other opportunities may be known to the local area agency on aging, the volunteer bureau, or the community fund.

In addition to or instead of volunteer activities, some people develop second and third careers after retirement. These may be an extension of the first career, but often they are quite different.

When Mrs. Farnsworth was retired from the public-school

system, having earlier completed the task of raising her children, she used the opportunity to realize a dream deferred. She had always wanted to teach kindergarten but had been unable to afford the time for the necessary preparation. With the aid of her church, she was able to get both the training and a job in a voluntary kindergarten. Several years later, when arthritis made it too difficult for her to keep up with the active five-year-olds, she began working on still another long-cherished plan—creative writing. She soon found herself involved in editing a community newsletter and, when time allowed, working on a book. Her experience illustrates how interests and abilities not used in the earlier career may get their chance for development later.

There is also a retirement from household responsibilities by both men and women. This is usually more gradual, less dramatic and traumatic, than retiring from work outside the home. After all, taking the garbage out or locking up at night does not stop at age sixty-five any more than does the cooking, the dusting, the cleaning. When the necessity to give up these tasks arrives, it can create its own kind of panic, but that is usually a later story, and is related to health rather than to any specific age. It does, however, illustrate the fact that the relinquishing of an accustomed role, for whatever reason, is likely to create a change in one's sense of who one is and what one is worth.

Whether for reasons of health, basic personality structure, or changes in their felt needs, some people, rather than increasing their activities after retirement, really prefer to sit and do nothing. Perhaps because our activist society sees little virtue in contemplation, they may be seen as "disengaged" and useless. But the life of the mind does not cease when the body becomes less active, even though it may change in focus.

A seventy-eight-year-old retired teacher was able to articulate the meaning of this change for her. She had been a very active and giving person in her professional career, and after retirement had continued this role as a volunteer tutor. But eventually she found that the volunteer activities no longer fulfilled her needs. Instead, she began keeping a diary and tried her hand at sketching. Sometimes she slept late; other days she woke up early and took long walks. She found pleasure in staring into the flames in the fireplace and letting her thoughts ramble. She called it "exploring the inscape."

Older societies have institutionalized the contemplative role for their elders. In India and the Near East, it is common for one who has completed his productive career to become a "holy man" or "possessor of wisdom." In the United States, development of different roles after the completion of child-rearing and breadwinning careers is more individual, perhaps an almost sub-rosa achievement. It tends not to be noticed or supported by society as a whole. This lack of automatically available, socially sanctioned roles can make post-retirement a lonely, frightening, and depressing time. For those able to create anew, however, it can be an exciting and rewarding time as well. One of the tasks that become more pressing as life spans lengthen and the over-sixty-five population increases is to pay more attention to the needs of the second half of life and how these are actually met. They may not always be best fulfilled by prolonging the previous roles, any more than the needs of adolescents are fulfilled by prolonging the activities of childhood. Giving thought to what one wants to do with the later years may make retirement, when it comes, a more enhancing and less threatening experience.

Changing Living Standards: Loss of Income

Retirement not only means loss of role, it usually also means loss of income. Although the retirement of Mr. Benson, the executive, was not a financial disaster, for most workers the reduction of income caused by retirement is very real. Combined with inflation, it may precipitate a drastic plunge into near poverty. This may be a more difficult adjustment for the relatively affluent than for those who have always been poor and are now poorer. But for all, it means a reduction of available options: the amount and kind of food one may eat; the choice of housing; the availability of medical care. Trips, impulsive treats, toys for grandchildren may have to be omitted or curtailed. In a society of rising expectations, where more and more of everything is the measure of success, such limitations mean not only material deprivation but a painful loss of selfhood.

Miss O'Brien spent her working life as a buyer for a retail clothing firm. When a series of illnesses forced her retirement and exhausted her savings, she was left with only her Social Security benefits to live on. Although three hundred dollars a month was much higher than the income of many of her contemporaries, Miss O'Brien found its limitations well-nigh intolerable: giving up a trusted family physician for the impersonality of a clinic; forgoing beauty-parlor appointments; being unable to give birthday and holiday gifts to nieces and nephews. She bitterly resented the governmental subsidies provided for those poorer than she— why was *she* not "deserving"?

Miss O'Brien's situation illustrates that retirement is not

the only cause of poverty among the old. Chronic illness can exhaust the savings of even the most frugal. Widowhood may cut a formerly manageable income in half, and leave the survivor not only bereft but unable to pay the rent. And for all, inflation contributes to the shrinkage of whatever resources are available.

It is a conservative estimate that a third of the 23,500,000 Americans over sixty-five live below the poverty line, on incomes of $3,500 or less per year. The inflation spiral is particularly hard on retired people, because their incomes are fixed but their living costs are not. Rent subsidies help some people to keep expenses in line with assets, but waiting lists are enormous. Meanwhile, it is not unusual for old people to spend half or more of their income for rent. Health care is another major expense, often a huge one. Those over sixty-five make more visits to doctors, have more hospitalizations, and buy more medications than those who are younger. In addition, they are more likely to need prosthetic devices to help compensate for physical deficits—hearing aids, dentures, glasses, walkers, or wheelchairs. All of these are expensive, and Medicare has been paying less and less of the total as medical costs continue to spiral. The state may pick up most of the bill for those eligible for public assistance, although there are limitations on the kind and amount of medication and treatment that will be paid for. Those above the eligibility line, defined differently in different states, may not be able to get any sort of assistance, yet have expenses that far exceed their means. They are often faced with hard decisions: is it necessary to give up a pleasant and familiar apartment or a long-standing relationship with a family doctor? Which is more important for a heart patient—her medicine or an elevator building? If she cannot afford both, she may opt to buy the medicine and curtail her activities so as to avoid stairs as much as possible. This course may lead to isolation, immobility, and depression; the opposite course may lead to an early death, or at least to very frequent hospitalizations. Ironically, the cost of hospital care, which is much higher than that of outpatient care, is usually covered in full by Medicare or private insurance, whereas outpatient expenses are apt to be covered minimally, if at all. The medical-insurance system thus reduces incentive and ability to use outpatient services and contributes to the overcrowding of hospitals and to the consequent increase in hospital costs. The brunt of this illogical approach is borne by the patients least able to afford it.

The Social Security system, the main source of income for most of those over sixty-five, also contains built-in contradictions. As the proportion of elderly to younger people increases, we hear rumblings about increases in the Federal Insurance Contributions Act (FICA) tax and the danger of bankrupting the program as benefits exceed contributions. Yet mandatory retirement and restrictive hiring policies force more and more senior citizens to become recipients. The net effect is to put additional stress on a public program, while restricting, rather than enhancing, the financial status of the individuals who are the intended beneficiaries.

The plight of retired people is that they find their incomes curtailed just when their expenses are increasing. This burden falls most heavily on those who are not poor enough for welfare but not rich enough to be totally self-sufficient. What do they do?

The most common solutions are savings and family help. But savings dwindle fast in a period of inflation, and catastrophic or chronic illness can quickly exhaust the savings of a lifetime. Although children are not legally required to contribute to the support of their parents, they very often do so if they can. However, this younger generation is also affected by inflation, and is likely to be still financing the care and education of those even younger, their own children, for whom they *are* financially responsible.

Retirement, Inflation, and the Middle Generation

The elderly, beset by so many changes, may find it difficult to understand that their children are dealing with changes, too. The middle generation may have their own kind of panic, which stems from their efforts to juggle so many simultaneous responsibilities. Sometimes the younger family may even begin to deal with their own retirement while still coping with the needs of their young and the changing needs of their old relatives. The necessity to determine their own priorities under these circumstances may well take on the proportions of a crisis.

Mrs. Henry was eighty-five when her son Martin and her daughter Janet's husband, Jim, retired. As they had long planned to do, Janet and Jim moved to Florida. Meanwhile, Martin developed emphysema. His doctor recommended a warm, dry climate. He and his wife resettled in Arizona. Mrs. Henry, in poor health and nearly blind, was left alone in Indiana with no immediate family nearby. She might perhaps have gone with one child or another, but she preferred to live out her life in a familiar place.

On the other hand, Mrs. Stein's only son, his wife, and their three children decided to move to Israel to start a new life, and asked Mrs. Stein to come with them. Her attitude was positive: "Of course, I'll go. My grandchildren and I are the future heritage of our people," she said. However, she was back in America within three months, resettled in her old neighborhood. She still felt close to her children, she said with breaking voice, because "we are good correspondents," but she was only at home here.

The dilemma faced by Mrs. Henry, Mrs. Stein, and their children is a real one. Should the children, now "old" themselves, have given up their plans and perhaps jeopardized their health and dreams? Should Mrs. Henry have uprooted herself to join her family? Should she have given up her own apartment and entered an institutional "home"? Should Mrs. Stein not have tried to move? Should she not have returned to the neighborhood, but gone into a "home," as insurance against the day when, without familiar supports, her failing health would demand a caretaking situation?

The available answers often seem to add up to deprivation, and denial of the needs of at least one person. What is increasingly clear is that society provides few supports for the job of growing old. The social institutions of the frontier have not yet caught up with the jet age.

Nevertheless, a beginning has been made. In many communities efforts are under way to increase the independence and security of old people without resorting to institutions. Existing resources can usually be located through state and local departments on aging. More will be developed as pressures to meet the needs increase. Families no longer make their own soap and candles, nor can the quality of life be guaranteed by individual efforts alone.

New Sources of Income for the Elderly

Some programs to improve the economic situation of elderly people have recently come into existence. Since they are new, many people are not aware of them.

Many states now grant property-tax rebates to older homeowners and renters alike. These rebates often amount to several hundred dollars. To learn whether your state has such a program, check with the state revenue department or the area agency on aging. Some states have sales-tax rebates as well. Thousands of elderly people are surprised each year to learn that they have money coming. Other thousands have not yet heard and may well be missing an opportunity.

A recent change in the tax law benefits older property owners. As of 1979, those over the age of fifty-five who sell their homes are exempt from capital gains tax on the first $100,000. This allows those who wish to move from a house to an apartment to do so without penalty.

Free or low-cost transportation is another popular form of income augmentation. The details vary from one locality to another. Discounts on a variety of other services are sometimes available, including, but not limited to, haircuts, veterinarians' fees, dental care, fishing licenses, and various recreational facilities. Because of the variety, locating any specific opportunity may require some detective work. The local authorities in charge of transportation, parks, or whatever service one is looking for may be able to provide information on discounts or special opportunities for the aged. Community referral services and any agencies specifically serving the elderly, such as senior citizens' centers, should be checked. Some newspapers have a department of public information or resource-finding. Churches and synagogues often sponsor, or know about, programs benefiting old people. To search out all the possibilities in a particular locality may be a formidable task for one individual, but locating and using someone who is knowledgeable about community resources can make the project less bewildering and more productive. Persistence, optimism, and a touch of luck help, too. (Agencies listed in Appendix III provide some guidelines.)

Housing Versus Inflation

Low-cost housing is one of the best hedges against inflation for those lucky enough to secure it. True, the demand for senior citizens' housing far exceeds the supply. In addition to buildings specifically constructed for the elderly, however, there are various forms of rent-subsidy and housing assistance. Most of these are funded by the Department of Housing and Urban Development (HUD), which can supply information on specific opportunities. A few have private or local funding, and those would be known only to the community where they exist.

Sharing expenses, either with family or with someone else, is another way of reducing housing costs. Old people sometimes move in with children or other relatives when they can no longer afford to maintain their own living quarters. Sometimes this works out well; sometimes it makes everybody miserable. The life styles of the older and younger generations may not mix very well, and may leave both parties feeling restricted and put upon. It may be easier to work things out with an unrelated roommate. Whether the sharing is with family or nonfamily, however, it helps to have a clear understanding, in advance, of what the expectations are. Not only how expenses are to be divided, but household responsibilities, use of kitchen and bathroom (when and for how long), entertaining, noise level, and preferred sleeping times need to be clarified. If one prospective roommate goes to bed early and rises at dawn to bird-watch, while the other stays up to watch the late, late, late show, they probably will not be very congenial!

Pensions

Social Security benefits are the most familiar form of pension income for retired people. Insurance and private pensions or union benefits may augment this. Sometimes private pensions are overlooked because they were earned many years before retirement. It is worthwhile for retired people to review their work history and determine whether they qualify for pensions for previous jobs. Pension plans sponsored by private industry or unions may also include survivors' benefits, so it is also important for widows to make sure they are getting all the monies to which they are entitled.

Veterans' benefits are another source of income sometimes overlooked. Not only the veteran but his or her dependents or survivors may be eligible. An allowance for assistance to the homebound, or for nursing-home care, may be available to those in need of such services. Because the application process can be a complicated one, some veterans' organizations offer help with it.

Assistance Programs

People on marginal incomes may be eligible for one of the public assistance programs. Supplemental Security Income (SSI) can be applied for through any Social Security office. It is intended to help those whose Social Security benefits are very small, and who may only have modest assets (up to $1,500). Public assistance grants are another possible source of income. Those who do not qualify for money grants may still be eligible for food stamps, medical assistance, or other special services such as household help.

Not everyone whose needs exceed his assets is eligible for any existing program, and even those who are may find their benefits beggared by inflation. Despite the resources of this most affluent society, all too often the solution to the discrepancy between assets and needs is doing without. The results may be inadequate diet, substandard housing, or second-rate health care. If not these essentials, then new clothes, an outing with friends, or entertaining the grandchildren may have to be sacrificed. It is probably resentment at having to do without, in an affluent society to which one has made lifelong contributions, that is responsible for much of the depression of old age. The big losses of health or spouse or old friends are not as eroding to self-esteem as the daily reminders of the low value that our society places on its aged members.

The restricted incomes available to the elderly are sometimes further curtailed by the reluctance of old people themselves to take advantage of benefits to which they are entitled, or of help which their families are willing and able to give them. This reluctance may stem from unwillingness to accept "charity," fear of losing independence, or dread of becoming "a burden." Whatever their cause, such feelings are sometimes a factor in increasing poverty among the aged.

The elderly and their children may benefit by the example of the various social and political groups which have learned how to lobby for public recognition of their needs. As the aged citizens increase in number, their influence as a pressure group could be significant. If augmented by that of interested younger people, it might even be formidable. The impact of such pressures is indicated by new programs and changes in existing laws which benefit elderly citizens. Some of these changes have been noted in this chapter; others may be in effect even before this book is in print.

The Old as Suppliers of Income

Poverty is one of the chief hazards of old age, but not all old people are poor. The possessors of great wealth are also included in the elderly population. This is not because so many old people are wealthy but because so many wealthy people are old. They are frequently the benefactors not only of their own families but of the community as well. Through inheritance and gifts, they support medical research, universities, museums, and causes of all kinds. Even misers without family or social conscience pay taxes.

Providing income and services for others is not limited to the wealthy. Those of more modest means are also sources of support. Many grandparents set up educational funds for their grandchildren, or provide wedding gifts, trips, cars, or down payments on houses. Even those who are considered poor themselves make contributions. As any minister will attest, the elderly members of his congregation are often better tithers than the young. Old men and women frequently use part of their Social Security income to help a ne'er-do-well son or an ailing daughter, or put it aside in order to have "something to leave" their children or grandchildren. In times of family crisis, a grandparent may be the only one available to care for small children, to nurse the sick, or to provide the means to avert financial disaster.

Conflict Between Individual and Family Needs

As the young and needy look to their elders for support, the old may be faced with a dilemma: given limited resources, whose needs have priority? This is really the same dilemma as that faced by younger people trying to juggle the needs of their adolescent children and their elderly parents, and still make room for their own lives. The only difference is that it happens at a later time.

Mr. Rolfe had established a trust account for his grandson's education. The boy's parents were both working, but their combined incomes would not stretch to cover college expenses. Mr. Rolfe had enjoyed the thought of helping them with this, and the younger family was grateful to think that their son could be assured of going to college without having to worry about paying for it.

Then Mrs. Rolfe got sick. Her condition quickly deteriorated to the point where she needed twenty-four-hour care. Mr. Rolfe dreaded the thought of placing her in a nursing home, but could not afford to care for her at home unless he used the money he had set aside for his grandson. What should he do? If he used the money to care for his wife, would he be jeopardizing his grandson's future? On the other hand, was not his wife entitled to care and comfort in her last days? The young man, after all, had youth and health and time in his favor. Plenty of youngsters have gotten an education without benefit of largesse from Grandpa. But college costs are increasing, jobs are harder to find, and, in any case, the family would be disappointed. Mr. Rolfe didn't want to let them down, and he didn't want to neglect his wife. What to do? He felt that no matter what he did, he would be sorry.

After much anguish and soul-searching, he decided to use the money for his wife. The family was not as disappointed as he had feared they would be. After all, they, too, had been distressed by Mrs. Rolfe's illness and concerned about her welfare. The teenage grandson, who had not really thought much about life after high school, began to look more seriously at what he wanted to do with his future and how to plan for it. Losing Grandpa's legacy was a jolt to the family, but in coping with it they rediscovered their investment in each other.

People, young and old, are often more flexible, compassionate, and capable of growth than they give themselves credit for. Mr. Rolfe's dilemma turned out to be more resolvable than he thought. Another man might have chosen differently. Individual circumstances and temperaments differ so much that there can be no "right" or "wrong" answers, only those that feel right to the people concerned.

The Financial Implications of Remarriage

The remarriage of an elderly widow or widower is another choice that has financial as well as emotional consequences. Their grown children may welcome the new alliance because of the companionship and contentment it promises to the older couple, as well as the prospect of lessened responsibility on their own part. Yet even the most accepting may have questions. What will happen to Mother's Social Security benefits? What if Dad gets sick—will his new wife be willing to take care of him? Who will inherit—will the children of the previous marriages lose their inheritance to the new spouses? And if prospective spouses attempt to deal equitably with inheritance questions by means of prenuptial agreements, does this businesslike procedure somehow alter the emotional impact of the union?

In the marriage of an older couple, it is no longer assumed that "two can live as cheaply as one." Indeed, with the effect of inflation on all living expenses, particularly the astronomical increases in medical and insurance costs, it has become impossible even for *one* to live as cheaply as one! Most serious of all, until January, 1979, a widow forfeited the Social Security benefits from her previous marriage if she remarried. (The same was true for widowers who claimed survivors' benefits.) This fact forced many old couples to choose between living in poverty and living in "sin." If they decided that they could not afford to marry because of the loss of income that would result, but chose to live together nonetheless, it was often at the cost of stirring up feelings of dishonesty and guilt in them and outrage in their associates.

In a younger couple, the question of weighing financial loss and emotional gain can be equated to the requirement that a divorced woman relinquish alimony upon remarriage. Cohabitation may be easier for the "liberated" younger generation than for old couples who would be violating a taboo in the moral code by which they were raised. It may be impossible for the older generation to accept either the thought of living together without legal and religious sanction or the thought of willingly undertaking a financial cutback. The need to maintain a sense of security through status and entitlements may have forced them to sacrifice the emotional security they found in their relationship.

It is heartening that this dilemma has finally been recognized and responded to by the lawmakers. As of January, 1979, widows' and widowers' benefits will no longer be stopped or reduced for those who remarry at age sixty or later, and previously reduced benefits to widows and widowers will be increased. These changes in the Social Security law should make decisions about remarriage somewhat easier.

For many families, however, the questions of estate and inheritance will continue to be thorny regardless of Social Security regulations. As in the Galt-Franklin romance (see page 22), the expectations of children may be in conflict with those of the new wife or husband, and the couple may feel compelled to choose between their relationship with their children and their relationship with each other. In the final analysis, perhaps it is a matter of where one chooses to find one's security and satisfaction. As usual, the solution that suits one couple will not necessarily fit everybody.

Assets: Mixed Blessing

The changes in life style that result from lost income or increased expenses may be greatest for those who have the most to lose. If one has had the means to live graciously and is reduced to penny-pinching, it is likely to be a difficult task to master, and a much resented one as well. Thus, Miss O'Brien (see page 36), found her retirement income gallingly inadequate, although it was twice as much as that of many of her contemporaries. She seethed with resentment at having to scrimp and save for shoes, new glasses, electricity, and dozens of other items that she had always taken for granted. She worried constantly about how she would get through the month, and was always short of money. Her next-door neighbor, whose income was much less, never seemed to have any trouble making it stretch. Having come to this country as an immigrant, and raised a family despite unemployment and the Depression, she had long since learned to manage on very little. Compared to the uncertainties of earlier years, she found her Social Security check a comfortingly predictable source of income. Living within it was no new task for her; indeed, it was an easier one than those she had coped with before.

It is not only that those who have more to lose have a harder time adjusting to the loss. The affluent often have to spend more for the same services than is expected from those of more modest means. For instance, many institutions still require that the applicant turn over all assets as a condition of admission, whether the assets amount to $5,000 or $50,000. Some nursing homes charge exorbitant rates and still expect families to pay for private-duty nurses. The rationale seems to be that "they can afford it," and that such payments make up for the lower profits provided by poorer patients. Thus those who have money are penalized for their success, and their estates may be lost to the families for whom they had planned to provide.

Those whose assets are relatively small may also find them a mixed blessing. If one spouse needs nursing-home care, for instance, the other spouse may be required to divest himself or herself of the joint assets of the couple in order to obtain admission eligibility. If Social Security income is also divided, the wife or husband who is still living in the community may be left virtually penniless. Some couples have resorted to divorce in order to avert this kind of pauperism.

The increased risk of chronic illness that goes with longer life spans does create a need for more nursing and personal care. It is essential to find ways of meeting the need without either reducing old people and their families to poverty or bankrupting the public treasury. The Medicare funding of home health agencies, which can provide some nursing care and assistance in the patient's home, is a step in this direction. It is by no means a complete answer, however, and we need to devise more creative and rational solutions to the cost-of-care problem. Citizens of any age, whether sick or well, need a way to be assured of comfort and dignity.

The Use of Money: A Personal Expression

For everyone, money is essential to survival. Yet the use one makes of money is as much an expression of personal style and basic character as is one's taste in food, music, friends, or recreation. A Miss O'Brien, for instance, would have as hard a time adopting her immigrant neighbor's economies as her neighbor would have understanding her need for pretty clothes, fresh flowers, or having her hair done.

Money serves many purposes. It may be used as a weapon, as a means of power over others, as security against time and change, as a means of denying one's plight, as a way to buy friendship, as a means of self-enhancement. One man may try to keep his children in line by threatening to cut them out of his will; another may feel that he can only maintain their interest by constant gifts. Both are using money as a means of control. The woman who skimps on food or clothing in order to add to her already substantial savings and the one who uses the rent money to buy a new dress are both denying reality. An elderly woman who was knocked down and injured in a robbery attempt barricaded herself in her apartment and spent most of her rent-rebate check on jimmy-proof locks for her doors and windows. Another, who suffered a similar experience, used her rebate check for an electric typewriter to compensate for the stiffness of her fingers. That had been her plan before the attack, and she saw no reason to change it despite her more threatened financial situation.

The ways in which people use money are affected by their earlier life experiences. The effects may be different, even opposite, for different people. Those who lived through the Depression, for instance, may be inveterate string-savers—frugal, cautious, and always worried about the future. Others, especially if they were children during the same period, may have grown up with the determination to see that *their* children should have all the things they felt deprived of. If the misers and the prodigals of the different generations are in the same family, they are likely to have a very difficult time understanding each other. For the old and young alike, their relationships and the quality of their lives are subject to personal and national economic fluctuations.

Perhaps the ninety-five-year-old woman who lived on dry bread and tea summed up the essence of money issues. When asked why she lived so frugally—what was she saving her money for—she replied, in all candor, "I'm saving it for my old age!"

3

Physical Changes: "The Spirit Is Willing but the Flesh Is Weak"

People in the later years of life find themselves contending with a variety of physical changes. These range from a general slowing down to serious illnesses that can be catastrophic in their effects. Weathering these successfully depends not only on good medical care but on the ingenuity and determination of the patient. The coping methods he has developed over the years are there to be used when new crises occur. In terms of dealing with problems, what has worked for him in the past will still work in the present, because the fact that his problem is new or different does not change the nature of the person who is dealing with it.

Insistence on Survival: Coping with Catastrophic Illness

Margaret McClendon was seventy-nine, a widow without children. She had supported herself for many years by various factory and domestic jobs, and had accumulated some savings. By the time she retired, she had a little house with flowers in front and vegetables behind, and she augmented her Social Security income by baby-sitting. In her church, she was an active matriarch who saw that things were done "right." One March day, on her way to the bus stop, she fell. The ambulance took her to the nearest hospital. She had had a stroke.

After some weeks in the hospital, Mrs. McClendon was to be discharged to a nursing home. The doctors said she could not take care of herself. But Mrs. McClendon thought otherwise. "I have a home," she said, "and I'm going to live in it." Against the opinion of experts, she went home. Neighbors and a few relatives helped, but no one was available to stay all the time. Since Mrs. McClendon could not get out of bed by herself, it became obvious that sporadic care was not enough.

One of the relatives got in touch with a social work agency, in the hope of getting Mrs. McClendon to be "more realistic." The social worker suggested a rehabilitation hospital, and helped Mrs. McClendon to apply. When she was admitted, the doctors felt there was little chance for improvement. She was seventy-nine years old, after all, and her balance was poor. Although they did not tell her so, they suspected that an inoperable brain tumor was responsible for her difficulty, and that it would only get worse. Again they recommended a nursing home. This time Mrs. McClendon got mad. "How do you know I can't get up unless you let me try?" she stormed. "Besides, if anybody falls, it will be me—so what are you all worried about?" She won a reprieve, and set about learning how to transfer from bed to wheelchair, from wheelchair to toilet. After six weeks, she had succeeded well enough to go home. She arranged to rent her house to a young family, retaining her bedroom and the use of the kitchen and bathroom. And she began, once again, to organize the community.

The qualities that had made her a formidable power in the Ladies Aid Society stood her in good stead now. She found someone to shop, to clean, to give her a bath, to change the bed, to shampoo her hair, to tend the garden and fix things. Her tongue was sometimes sharp, and she was not above arm-twisting. But she was always careful to have two or three people for each task, so that no one should be overburdened. "My mama used to tell me," she would say, " 'don't ride a gift horse to death.' "

As her strength increased, she learned to push her wheelchair as a combined walker and carrying basket. She reserved her real walker for trips outdoors when she didn't have to carry anything. She was able to resume her church activities by getting a ride and having two men carry her in on a chair. Once inside, she was as matriarchal as ever, with a sharp eye for laxity in any form. "Young man," she might say to a fifty-year-old usher, "when did you last shine your shoes?"

Mrs. McClendon had strong political opinions, and when a constitutional referendum was called, she was determined to get to the polls and vote. Getting a ride was no problem, but the polling place was in a school. This meant negotiating a long half-block of winding sidewalk, a shallow flight of stairs, two heavy doors, and a corridor running the length of the building. For most voters, getting to the gym where the polling booths were set up was a five-minute walk. For Mrs. McClendon, it was forty-five minutes of concentrated effort.

In *Death Be Not Proud,* John Gunther movingly describes his son's graduation march—a quarter-mile hike for the seventeen-year-old Johnny, who was within two weeks of his death from a brain tumor. He had kept up with his class through a year and a half of almost constant hospitalization and had maintained his balance, coordination, and vision only through fierce determination. His father describes the crescendo of applause by those who watched that heroic achievement.[1] Margaret McClendon, struggling down the last few steps of that long school corridor, was also achieving what the doctors had said was impossible. But for her there was no cheering section—only the anxious poll workers hurrying out to offer her a chair and a drink of water. Why is it that when an old person thumbs his nose at fate and succeeds, one's first reaction is apt to be "Oh, but you shouldn't have!" instead of "Bravo!"?

Slowing Down

It is not only the major rehabilitation efforts that demand energy and persistence. Dealing with the many insidious physical effects of declining health requires its own kind of heroism.

As the human body grows older, everything slows down. The trip to the store that was once accomplished in twenty minutes now takes an hour. One eighty-year-old expressed her frustration with her aging body: "I'm O.K. but my feet won't walk." Too proud to ask younger folk to slow their pace to hers, she always told them, "I walk so slowly, you go on ahead. And," she told the interviewer sadly, "they always do." In a society that values speed, the slowing of reflexes is not only frustrating but alienating as well. Just as deafness is often equated with stupidity, so a decrease in speed may be equated with incompetence. Such assumptions may be holdovers from childhood when bigger children lorded it over smaller ones—"Yah! You don't talk right . . . you're always tagging along. . . . You're too little to play with us." The appearance of clumsiness, slowness, or any other lack of physical prowess can evoke painful anxiety in both the less able and in their observers.

One of the disadvantages of our society's technological development is the fact that the human body can seldom keep pace with the machine. This discrepancy increases with age and may make it difficult or impossible for old people to take advantage of automation, not just in work situations but in their personal lives as well.

Mr. Daniels, age seventy-three, had been driving since he was twelve. There was no minimum age in those days. In his late sixties, he developed Parkinson's disease, but still continued to drive despite the shaking of his hands. One Saturday afternoon he lost his balance and fell down a flight of stairs. This experience frightened Mr. Daniels badly, and his wife even more. They decided that it was time for him to give up driving. Mr. Daniels became severely depressed over this loss of mobility and autonomy. Although his physical condition had not really changed, he felt like an invalid. Before many weeks had passed, he was in a nursing home. The staff could not figure out why he was there—or why he was so irascible.

Mr. Daniels was a victim of double jeopardy. He no longer had the quick reflexes needed for coping with modern traffic, and in losing the ability to control a car, he had lost one of the greatest modern symbols of power and manhood. This made him feel useless and incompetent—a fact that was confirmed for him by the subsequent institutionalization.

One of the ways of dealing with the slowing-down process is to build in more time. A shopping trip can become a leisurely event rather than a hasty and harried one. So can other activities. One elderly gentleman took to getting up a few hours earlier each morning, in order to dress, shave, and complete his exercises in an unhurried fashion.

In this age of super-jets, when it is possible to cross a

continent in five hours without seeing any of it, taking more time can provide us with the opportunity to actually look at our surroundings and savor our experiences. The old may discover, and perhaps even teach the young, that speed is not really essential to the enjoyment of life.

Whether one is attempting rehabilitation after a major illness or only adjusting to the slower pace of an aging body, it is important to remember that old dogs can indeed learn new tricks—but it takes longer.

The Frustration of Decreasing Control

Decrease in physical stamina means less control over one's environment. How ridiculous a competent cook feels when because her arthritic fingers can no longer manipulate a can opener, an essential ingredient in her recipe is inaccessible. How infuriating to be the helpless victim of an inanimate object—and such a small one! The weight of a vacuum cleaner and the height of bus steps likewise make formerly simple tasks difficult. In coping with these changes, ingenuity often replaces dexterity. One woman, nearly blind from glaucoma, explained how she knew when her gas stove was properly lit. "I hear the 'poof!' " she said. "If I don't hear it, I turn it off again." Another, whose hands were too stiff to wring out a sweater, rolled it in a towel and sat on it— truly a rear-guard action!

Sensory Changes

It is not only that the human machine slows down and becomes less responsive to the demands upon it. The senses through which we keep in touch with the world become less acute, less able to provide us with information.

At a Thanksgiving gathering, twenty people were talking at once. Auntie Lou described her Grand Canyon trip to Cousin Ann while Uncle Ted and Uncle Jack exchanged fishing stories. Grandpa Jennings struggled to untangle the threads of competing conversations, turning from one to the other and adjusting his hearing aid. Finally he gave up in disgust. "I don't see why you young people have to mumble so. People don't speak clearly anymore. In my day, we were taught to speak up." He wandered over to watch grandsons Mark and Harry play checkers, a game which requires no acuteness of hearing. He patted the boys' heads, then sat down in a corner. A half-grown kitten plunked itself on his lap, and he stroked it absently.

Grandpa Jennings's shift from listening to watching and stroking as his means of communication was consistent with both his liabilities and his assets. Sensory changes redefine the world for elderly people. Hearing loss may result in the lessening of effort to relate to others, may produce discouragement or disinterest, or, in its extreme, may account for impaired judgment. In a party atmosphere, the aging eye may adjust poorly to lower light frequency, and eating by candlelight may soon lose its charm. As nerve endings thicken, taste and smell sensations are dulled, and Grandpa Jennings is not consoled by the culinary delights of the holiday celebration. Instead, he relies for comfort on that capacity which has not decreased with age—his sense of touch and the pleasurable sensation of stroking and caressing.

The decreasing acuteness of sight and hearing is an encroachment on the older person's control of his life. The blurred vision that results from cataracts may virtually eliminate such activities as reading and sewing. Identifying labels in a store, crossing streets safely, and even determining whether a floor is dusty or a dress needs washing become difficult tasks. Hearing loss makes conversation difficult to follow, especially in groups, and this often leads to increased isolation. Those who have had major losses of sight or hearing often become unreasonably suspicious. They fear that others are talking about them, laughing at them, planning to take advantage of them. The specific fears may be unfounded, but what is very real is the sense that one's perceptions of the world are faulty and unreliable. Suspiciousness is an attempt to protect oneself from dependence on the unknown—as much a reflex as flinching from a blow.

Learning to compensate for the particular disability is a means of restoring a measure of control, and with it the security of once more feeling at home in the world. It should go without saying that the cause of impairment should always be medically determined and treated insofar as possible. For example, two of the most common causes of visual impairment among the elderly are cataracts and glaucoma. Cataracts can often be corrected by surgery and special glasses. This is a time-consuming procedure, since the eyes require a period of healing and adjustment before the glasses can be used. One who is contemplating or has undergone cataract surgery is likely to need a lot of reassurance and support, as well as practical help during convalescence. The fact that vision gets worse before it gets better can be very frightening. When the improvement does come, however, the resulting gains in independence can justify all the time and anxiety expended.

Glaucoma is a more insidious sight-stealer, because in the early stages there is no pain or any change in the appearance of the eyes. It can be diagnosed by a very simple and painless test, which should be part of the routine examinations of all elderly people—indeed, of all people over forty. If diagnosed early, it can be arrested and controlled by medication, but untreated glaucoma is a leading cause of blindness.

Hearing impairment can often be improved by hearing aids or other treatment. These should always be prescribed by a doctor, preferably one who has access to the services of a competent audiologist. Far too many elderly people have wasted money on ill-fitting or ineffective hearing aids touted by glib salesmen. The prescription and proper fitting of a hearing aid is a sophisticated medical procedure; it is not like buying aspirin or Band-Aids.

Sometimes, unfortunately, there is no treatment that can restore function, or the restoration is very limited. There are, however, often other means available to help compensate for the deficits. Classes in lip-reading may be available for the hard-of-hearing. Families may be taught how to communicate more easily with the member who has a hearing loss. Even those who have not had formal instruction in lip-reading can usually hear better if they can see the face of the person who is talking. Indeed, most of us can hear better when we can see—like the music lover who always takes opera glasses to the symphony or the lady who cannot answer the telephone comfortably without putting on her glasses. Speaking slowly rather than loudly gives the hard-of-hearing person a better chance to understand. An amplifier may be attached to the telephone, or a doorbell with an especially loud ring installed. Light signals are sometimes used to attract a deaf person's attention to a doorbell or oven buzzer.

The blind and near-blind may be eligible for mobility training, either from one of the associations for the blind or from the state. Such training can enable a person to get around outdoors and to use public transportation with the aid of a special cane. Instruction in Braille is available for those with the motivation and finger sensitivity to undertake it. Talking books can help restore the pleasures of reading. The visually handicapped can also be helped to organize their homes so as to find things readily by touch. Self-adhering ribbon known as Velcro sewn to the inside of a dress can identify its color and make accessories easier to organize. Bits of felt glued to medicine bottles in varying patterns can be used to distinguish one from another—an essential safety measure for those who must take several different medications daily. The use of large print and good, nonglare lighting can help one to make the most of his remaining vision and to enhance enjoyment. Sunglasses may be helpful if eyes are sensitive to glare and may make accidents less likely. An electric stove may be easier and safer to use than gas; however, those who do not have electric stoves may, as we have noted, learn to substitute hearing for sight and determine by sound whether the stove is properly lit. Of course, if hearing is also a problem, this solution will not work very well. Those who suffer from multiple deficits need a special measure of ingenuity and help to maintain contact with the world.

Perhaps the most effective means of communication is touch. Even those who cannot see or hear or remember can respond to a firm handclasp or a hug. Touching tells people that they are not alone, that they are still valuable members of society. Solitary confinement is a punishment reserved for the worst criminals—it should not be imposed on the elderly!

The Diseases of Aging Are Treatable

Miracle drugs and improved health care have brought us a longer life span and better control of acute illness.

But in the additional years there can also be increased incidence of the degenerative diseases: cancer, diabetes, Parkinsonism, heart disease, strokes, arthritis. It should be em-
phasized that although the risk of such illnesses is higher
in the later years, illness is not part of the aging process
nor is it caused by old age. No one dies of old age. It is
not "normal" to be sick at any age, and treatment must
be provided at all ages.

༃ Most older people and their families are well aware of
the hazards to health, and their reactions range from apathy
("I'm old, so what can you do?") to acute fearfulness and
constant demand for medical attention. Often, once a diagnosis is established, the patient assumes that all his symptoms of discomfort can be ascribed to it. However, with
old people as well as with younger ones, it is important
to remember that symptoms change, and that awareness
of these changes is more important in the understanding
of the patient's health than is the knowledge of his diagnostic label. As a pediatrician finds a description of tempera-
ture, cough, pain, or listlessness more useful than the statement that "my child has a cold," so an older person's
physician is helped by reports of change in his patient's
condition. Noting such change and reporting it to the physician are more useful in promoting good health care than
studying and addressing specific disease entities could ever
be.

A word of caution: this general discussion of the diseases
of aging is intended only as a guide to alert patients and
their families to possible trouble spots and treatment needs,
not as a substitute for consultation with a doctor. It is well
to remember that "a little learning is a dangerous thing."
A layman's interpretation of fragmentary information can

be disastrous if it results in the nontreatment of treatable
conditions. One should not practice medicine without a li-
cense, even on oneself.

The Hazards of Overmedication

One of the complications of treating the diseases of old
age is that sometimes the alleviation of one problem creates
another. For instance, medication taken for arthritis may
produce ulcers, and many medicines in combination, or
too high dosage, may produce the appearance of confusion
and senility. It is estimated that many hospitalizations of
the elderly are caused by overmedication. It is not surprising
that this is so, since one person may be taking, simultaneously, medications to control high blood pressure, diabetes, heart pain, and water retention, plus, perhaps, an anti-
depressant or a tranquilizer. Furthermore, while old people
are likely to be taking more medicines than younger people,
they have a lower tolerance for high dosages, and may need
a much smaller amount of a particular drug than would
usually be prescribed for a younger person. An experienced
geriatric physician often told his students: "If you think
Mrs. Jones is confused, try taking her medications for a week
and see how *you* feel." It is desirable that elderly people
be treated by doctors who are familiar with geriatric problems; it is essential that any doctor be kept informed of
all the medicines his patient is taking. In this age of special-
ization, when several different doctors may be prescribing
for one person, this task in itself may require a route sheet!
Besides, the patient may well be taking over-the-counter
remedies that do not require a prescription, yet may inter-
act with his other medications, causing unanticipated side

· effects. Truly, the maintenance of good health becomes a formidable task in old age.

Reluctance to Seek Treatment

It is not unusual for the elderly to fail to seek, or to ignore, their doctors' advice because the degree of alleviation they can expect to gain seems too small to be worth the bother of treatment. A diabetic, for instance, may find the balance of food and insulin in the system very difficult to achieve, even with the most meticulous observance of diet. When self-discipline provides so uncertain a result, the temptation to indulge in forbidden sweets and snacks may be irresistible. Or a heart patient, advised by the doctor to "take it easy," may ignore the advice.

Mrs. Cahill was such a patient. When she felt fairly well, she *would* clean house—play with her grandchildren—go downtown to shop. Then, in all likelihood, she would have a severe attack of breathlessness and heart pain, resulting in an emergency trip to the hospital. However, Mrs. Cahill maintained that she got those attacks anyway, and why waste her good days by sitting still?

It is also not uncommon that people are shy about reporting symptoms or asking questions, and they often don't do so because they don't want to appear "stupid." They feel that "the doctor is so busy" that questions are an encroachment on his time. There is, unfortunately, often some truth to the accusation that there are doctors who do not consider elderly patients interesting or worthwhile, or that some resist devoting their time to chronic ailments from which no dramatic recovery is anticipated. This is a part of the message that our society gives to the elderly: if they can't be young, they should be decently invisible (an ironic reversal of the old-fashioned dictum that *children* should be seen and not heard).

Another aspect or perhaps result of this attitude is that many elderly people feel embarrassed about their disabilities. The tremor of Parkinsonism, for instance, may mean that one cannot manage a fork or balance a cup without spilling. Victims of the disease may give up eating in restaurants because they feel so conspicuous. Some are ashamed to eat in the presence of any others and therefore avoid even family gatherings. Another source of private agony is uncertainty about one's ability to control urine—or, worse yet, feces. Those who know they need to stay very close to toilet facilities may make all kinds of excuses for avoiding trips and family outings. "I don't feel good today." "It's too far to Janet's." "Movies are terrible these days." Such reactions may be put down to the crotchets of age, when actually they are the result of acute embarrassment.

The Fear of Deterioration

It can be said that everybody has something to hide. Children pretend to be older than they are, in an attempt to avoid the stigma of childishness. Adolescents agonize over acne and awkwardness, the speed of physical development or lack thereof. Young adults, faced with the responsibility of home and career, conceal their uncertainty. Older adults try to hide their doubts and second thoughts about the way they have conducted their lives, or their impulses to kick over the traces. And the oldest adults hide their physical deterioration; at least they hide it from themselves. "Everybody mumbles," complains Grandpa Jennings as he fiddles with his hearing aid. But many oldsters (and youngsters, too) refuse to wear a hearing aid at all, preferring instead to pretend that they hear as well as ever. Canes, glasses, talking books, grab bars, and other devices to compensate for physical deficits may be impatiently rejected. This seeming unreasonableness is probably due to the dread of old age as a time of helplessness and worthlessness, which is so strongly reinforced by our youth-worshiping culture. The earliest signs of physical decline are interpreted as a harbinger of worse things to come. Andrew Marvell expressed it this way in "To His Coy Mistress":

> But at my back I always hear
> Time's wingèd chariot hurrying near . . .

When one assumes that old age can only mean loss, ugliness, incompetence, and the scorn of others, even the discovery of a gray hair can send a shiver up the spine, as from a chill wind out of the abyss of time.

Expecting Too Little or Too Much

Because there are such wide variations in stamina and skill, and because these change over time for any individual, it is hard both for old people and for their families to know how much to expect. This is particularly difficult when an older person wants to do either more or less than his or her associates think is suitable.

So it was when seventy-five-year-old Ellie Hopkins decided to take swimming lessons at the local Y.M.C.A., and applied to her doctor for a permit. He was incredulous. "Why do you want to swim at your age?" he asked. Ellie didn't think that was any of his business, but he was so insistent that she finally snapped, "Well—I'll tell you. My mother swims—and it just embarrasses me to death because

I can't!" The doctor's jaw dropped. "How old is your mother?" he finally managed to ask. "Oh," replied Ellie, "she'll be a hundred her next birthday."

She got her swimming lessons. The doctor, we hope, got a lesson in the fact that human individuality is not age-bound.

On the other hand, those experiencing progressive disabilities may be totally frustrated when they are expected to continue to function as they always have. Such unrealistic demands may precipitate further withdrawal, and discourage the efforts that the handicapped person might still be able to make.

Mrs. Kramer developed a muscular weakness which made it increasingly more difficult to swallow and to talk. Her family's conclusion was: she's withdrawing, we mustn't let her; she should get involved in the community center, be with people. Mrs. Kramer didn't want that. Being in a group intensified her awareness of her speech problem. She painfully articulated her feelings about herself to the social worker at the center: "I *was* a person." Her depression was due not only to her loss of function but also to her perception that, because of it, she was no longer herself. What she needed was not a group, but *one* person who would be willing to listen until she got the words out, one by one. This was difficult for her family because of their dismay at her dysfunction. They kept trying to make her "like her old self," which only increased her depression. With the help of the social worker, a volunteer with some training in speech therapy was found to visit Mrs. Kramer. She was able not only to communicate with the old lady but to help her—although unable to improve her speech— to live more comfortably with the disability. The volunteer's acceptance of Mrs. Kramer's actual capabilities helped her to recover some of her self-esteem, and even to tolerate appearing in public places.

Mrs. Kramer's story illustrates how difficult it can be to find the fine line between expecting too little and expecting too much of a disabled person.

Circumventing Physical Defects

As physical strength decreases, the old person may be more willing to acknowledge difficulties and accept help if the abilities he or she still has are used and honored.

Martha Corning suffers from multiple sclerosis, has had frequent hospitalizations, and is confined to a wheelchair. Yet she has firmly resisted institutionalization. So far, she has been able to use the help of neighbors and a community nursing service to cope with her disabilities. In spite of severe bouts of illness, she has maintained her hobbies and an active social life. "I'm not handicapped," Martha insists, "but I'm inconvenienced." Her apartment is a greenhouse, and she is the building's acknowledged authority on growing plants. Neighbors drop in frequently to visit and to get her advice on what to do for an ailing cyclamen or a drooping African violet. Although they help Martha a great deal, they feel helped in return, which promotes both their willingness to give and Martha's self-esteem in accepting.

Another lady, whose infirmities keep her housebound, makes beautiful and original quilts. She has been offered large sums of money for them, but so far she has been too busy providing for grandchildren to cater to the open market.

Both ladies exemplify that the ingenuity displayed by many old people in overcoming or sidestepping the deficits of aging is impressive, indeed.

Outwitting the Symptoms

Not only can the remaining abilities be utilized, but often the disabilities can be reduced or at least made more tolerable. The necessary ally in such an approach is a competent doctor who is sympathetic to old people and optimistic about their chances. It is well worth the time to look for a doctor who is interested in helping people to cope with the caprices of their aging bodies. Reassurance and practical advice can often ease panic as well as reduce risk. Many of the symptoms which cause inconvenience, discomfort, or hazard can be alleviated or avoided, often by very simple means. For instance, the dizziness which makes older people easily subject to falls is likely to be the result of getting up too quickly: blood drains away from the brain, resulting in light-headedness or even blackouts. This problem can often be circumvented by moving *slowly* to a sitting and then to a standing position, allowing one's circulation the time to accommodate to the changes. (Pregnant women often experience the same phenomenon, and find the same remedy helpful.) Sometimes old people get up too quickly, especially at night, because of an urgent need to get to the bathroom. Using a night light and keeping a portable commode close to the bed may alleviate both the anxiety and the hazard.

The Need for Proper Foot Care

One hazard to mobility that is often overlooked is improper foot care. Because of decreased circulation to the feet and legs, old people are susceptible to foot injuries. Corns and calluses that are neglected, inexpertly trimmed at home, or treated with corn plasters can develop infections that are very slow to heal and that can even result in the loss of a limb. Diabetics are especially vulnerable but all elderly people should avoid home remedies for foot care, or even cutting their own toenails. The regular use of a podiatrist may be the ounce of prevention that maintains comfort and mobility and staves off serious disability.

Avoiding Falls

One of the most serious hazards to the mobility and independence of old people is fractures—especially broken hips. Although there are pathological fractures that occur spontaneously as the result of disease or malnutrition, most fractures are caused by falls, and most falls are avoidable. Some causes of falls, in addition to dizziness and painful feet, may be slippery floors, small throw rugs, poor lighting, and ill-fitting shoes. The solutions to these are obvious. Grab bars around the tub and toilet may prevent slips in the bathroom. Another cause of falls (and not only among the elderly!) is using chairs or other makeshift supports to reach high cabinets or other out-of-reach objects. Ideally, housing for the elderly (and, perhaps, the youngerly) should be so arranged that all storage space is within arm's reach. Of course, the houses and apartments where people actually live are seldom ideal. The hazards of climbing may be reduced by using long-handled tongs (i.e., for replacing light bulbs), sturdy stepladders, or, best of all, having someone else present to assist. Having to wait for the "someone else" is, however, one of the chief irritants of old age. It makes the organization of one's day dependent on another's schedule, and this provides a reminder of one's decreased ability to manage one's own environment. Small wonder that old people often prefer to defy circumstances and risk the danger, to the despair of their children, physicians, and well-wishers.

When Old People Insist on Taking Risks

Colette, in a recollection of her mother, describes the family's loving efforts to get the old lady to sit still and be waited on, and the mother's indignant resistance. One day she was "caught red-handed in the most wanton of crimes": sawing her own firewood, with "an indescribable expression of guilty enjoyment."[2] When the aging body no longer obeys orders reliably, the sweetest of forbidden fruits may be attempting some task that used to be easy. In so doing one defies time and change, and declares: "I am!"

Instead of attempting the impossible, old people sometimes achieve ingenious compromises. An American lady, about the same age as Colette's mother, had also been accustomed to chopping her own firewood at the family's summer cabin. At eighty-three, she reluctantly gave up this task, realizing that her arthritic hands no longer had a secure grip on the axe. Her solution was to pull up the dead saplings by the roots and break them over her knee! Like the lady who resorted to "sitting power" to wring out a sweater, her philosophy was "if one limb fails you, try another."

An eighty-five-year-old, worried about the weight of the snow on her sagging porch roof, achieved an equally original solution. She knew that she could no longer climb out on the roof to shovel the snow, so she opened the window above the roof and scooped as much as she could reach into a dishpan. She then carried the pan into the bathroom and dumped its contents into the tub to melt. A window squeegee attached to a mop handle enabled her to push the rest of the snow off the eaves. Having coped with blizzards in her youth, she was not about to be outwitted by a city snowstorm!

These two intrepid women illustrate not only the ingenuity that can go into coping with physical handicaps, but the fact that the solutions arrived at are not totally risk-free. Either lady could have slipped, strained her back, or encountered some other hazard. This fact often worries the families of the elderly, who long to keep them "safe." But total safety is not consistent with active functioning. Children who are protected from all risks never develop the ability to deal with them. The need to solve problems and master one's environment continues throughout life, and success in such endeavors is a prime ingredient in anyone's self-esteem. The problems and the solutions change, but to give up the search for solutions is to give up life itself.

For this reason, those who care for the elderly often have to achieve compromises between what seems medically desirable and what the old person is willing to accept. For instance, a young nurse discovered that one of her patients had a descending aortic aneurysm—a weak spot in a major artery. The lady's blood pressure was 240/180—so high that a break in the blood vessel seemed imminent. If it occurred, no treatment would be possible and death would be virtually instantaneous. The nurse wanted to call an ambulance immediately and get the patient to the hospital. The patient, however, would have none of it. She finally agreed to go to the hospital, but by herself—on a bus. The nurse, fearful that further agitation would raise the lady's blood pressure even higher, and perhaps bring on the condition she was trying to avert, reluctantly agreed. The lady reached the hospital without mishap, and was immediately admitted to intensive care, where she responded well to treatment. The attending physicians were horrified at the nurse's "negligence" in not calling an ambulance, but her supervisor, wiser in the ways of geriatric patients, reassured her. She said: "If they'd rather go safely in a wheelbarrow instead of recklessly in an ambulance—let them."

Easing Fatigue

A constant factor in the problem-solving process is fatigue. Tiring easily is one of the exasperations of aging. "The spirit is willing," as the saying goes, but the protesting body can't keep up. One very active seventy-seven-year-old, deeply involved in community affairs, complained to her doctor that she couldn't seem to stay up as late as she used to, and her feet were swelling. He advised her to get some more rest and to elevate her feet frequently during the day. "How can I keep my feet up?" she replied indignantly. "I have to get the newsletter out this week!"

Nevertheless, there are ways of continuing activity with less effort. A comfortable step stool in the kitchen may make cooking and dishwashing easier, and cabinet space may be arranged so as to save steps and reaching. The American Heart Association has a publication that can assist the housewife to reorganize her household tasks so as to conserve energy.[3]

Fatigue from prolonged walking or standing can often be eased by regular foot care and properly-fitting shoes. (An untended corn or a shoe that rubs or pinches can make one hurt all over!) The weariness of waiting for public transportation was avoided by one lady who used a small folding chair. When the bus came, she folded the chair, popped it into her shopping bag, and got aboard.

Pain and Stiffness: The Plague of Arthritis

A common enemy for many old people is arthritis. Its effects range from morning stiffness in some joints to almost total immobility and severe pain. Heat and aspirin are the standard remedies for pain, aspirin having the additional effect of reducing inflammation. Regular mild exercise helps to combat stiffness, since keeping the joints in motion prevents "freezing." Some community centers and senior citizens' clubs offer classes in body dynamics, which can be helpful in maintaining comfort and mobility.

It is essential to maintain mobility despite the discomfort that may be involved in doing so. Controlling arthritis depends more on the patient's interest in life and activity than on the actual extent of the disease.

One seventy-seven-year-old man, for instance, was accustomed to catching a trout every morning for the family breakfast. He would first secure enough grasshoppers to bait the hooks, which he then stuck into the brim of an ancient fishing cap. Darting about the yard in search of his prey, he looked rather like a grasshopper himself. He was by far the most successful fish provider in the family, a fact which he attributed to his exclusive use of fresh grasshoppers.

On a visit to his son, "Pop" complained that his legs bothered him a little. They consulted the son's doctor, who, after examining the x-rays, stated, "According to these, he can't walk a step—but I saw him walk into the office!"

The management of arthritis, like that of any disease, should be under a doctor's supervision. Because the condition is painful and there is no cure for it, people often resort to home remedies and amateur advice. Worse, they may resort to quacks who promise marvelous results from devices which are, at best, worthless, but always expensive. Since arthritis is a chronic disease which never kills anybody, it provides a rich opportunity for these unscrupulous cure-mongers.

For fingers stiffened by arthritis, many ordinary chores become extremely difficult. We have already referred to the lady who resorted to "sitting power" when her hands could not wring out a sweater. Jar lids, can openers, bottle caps also create obstacles. An electric can opener may be the solution, or if one is not available, a long-handled manual can opener with a large turning wheel. Tapping with a knife or spoon handle may help to break the vacuum in a jar lid. The law now permits druggists to provide standard rather than childproof caps for medications, but these must be specifically requested. If fingers cannot grip a thermometer, it can be shaken down by wrapping it in a towel and shaking the towel.

Arthritis sufferers could provide many other examples of the means they have devised for outwitting the enemy. Perhaps groups of them could compile their suggestions into a handbook, as good cooks share recipes. Some such handbooks already exist, such as an unpublished one compiled by the Visiting Nurses Association of Ann Arbor, Michigan, entitled, "Living Easy."[4]

Parkinsonism: Another Threat to Mobility

Victims of Parkinsonism, like arthritis, have problems grasping objects: their hands tremble uncontrollably, causing them to drop things. Not only is this a source of embarrassment, as we have noted earlier, but it also makes cooking and eating problematic. Nutrition may become inadequate because of the difficulty of preparing such foods as comprise a balanced diet. For those who live alone, reliance on pre-cooked foods may be a necessity. Sliding pans and dishes along a counter instead of lifting them may make food preparation easier and the use of a bent plastic straw can make lifting a cup or glass unnecessary. Lightweight and unbreakable dishes are also a help.

Another source of embarrassment to victims of Parkinsonism is the masklike expression which results from inability to control facial muscles. Unable to laugh or smile easily, they may be considered cranky and unresponsive by friends and family. Understanding the real cause of the problem can help both them and their associates to live with it more comfortably.

Despite the tremors and the poor balance which make falls a frequent occurrence, many patients continue to function independently for a fairly long time. One seventy-year-old who has diabetes in addition to Parkinsonism manages to get to a workshop every day, although she walks with difficulty and must use public transportation to get there. Because of the tremors, she has to have someone give her insulin shots, and needs to have cooked meals brought in. Yet she manages to maintain her apartment and continue her social activities. Her doctor thinks she should be in a nursing home but she will have none of it, and has put a great deal of energy and ingenuity into finding ways to protect her own life style.

Malnutrition: The Silent Enemy

Coping with the deficits of an aging body requires energy, and energy is what is most likely to be in short supply. It is often further sapped by a silent and unsuspected enemy: malnourishment.

We tend to associate poor nutrition with poverty. Although restricted income may be one reason for inadequate diet, it is not the only one. Some others are: lack of interest in and energy for cooking, especially for oneself; dislike of eating alone; missing teeth or poorly-fitting dentures that make chewing difficult; depression. Whatever the cause, the fact is that many elderly people tend to eat whatever is easiest to prepare, be it crackers and tea, sweet rolls, or dry cereal. Such diets are deficient in protein, vitamins, minerals, and roughage. Over a period of time they can result in constipation and other digestive disorders, bad teeth and brittle bones, dizziness and frequent falls, increased apathy and depression, and possibly the appearance of confusion and disorientation.

Being malnourished means being susceptible to many other diseases, and may show through a myriad of symptoms. Ironically, for instance, malnutrition may be associated with obesity. The empty calories pile on weight, which creates an additional strain on the heart and other organs, aggravates arthritis, and decreases mobility. If a person is suffering from some condition that requires a specific diet, as in diabetes, the situation becomes even more critical. It is estimated that there are many undiagnosed diabetics among the elderly because blood-sugar tests were not a matter of routine in medical examinations a few years ago. Uncontrolled diabetes can result in a comatose condition which might be mistaken for drug abuse or a stroke, or could manifest itself in agitated behavior that appears psychotic. If diagnosed correctly and in time, these symptoms can be eliminated by medication combined with proper diet.

A thorough medical checkup may also reveal an unsuspected condition whose treatment could help to make food more palatable again. For instance, if Father has been having pain after eating because of diverticulitis or ulcers, he will be understandably reluctant to face the dinner table. Once his pain is alleviated, the prospect of mealtime becomes much more attractive.

Properly fitted dentures can take the pain out of eating and have a profound effect not only on nutrition but also on self-esteem. People are less interested in eating, or anything else, when they feel ugly and decrepit. The restoration of the ability to manage food comfortably and look nice at the same time can create a new lease on life. The family may be amazed at how with-it Grandma has become since she got her new teeth!

Correcting poor dietary habits is not easy at any age. Parents of young children bewail their refusal to eat anything but hamburgers, hot dogs, and peanut butter. Adolescents consume chocolate bars and pizza, in defiance of acne. Harried businessmen and housewives alike try to subsist on black coffee and cigarettes. Elderly people are no more inclined to eat what they should than anybody else is. It is remarkable that in the richest country in the world, with the widest variety of foodstuffs available, so many people who could afford to do otherwise feed themselves so poorly. For instance, although calorie requirements are ten to fifteen percent lower for elderly people, their need for protein is even greater than that of growing adolescents. Osteoporosis, a brittle-bone condition which causes many fractures, can be reversed by large amounts of calcium, available in milk, dairy products, and green vegetables.

A person who is already apathetic about food is not likely to want to make the effort to change. (Consider how difficult it is to stick to a weight-loss diet, especially when you're feeling low!) Nevertheless, there are measures that can sometimes spark interest. Nutrition centers for the elderly where hot meals are served at a modest price attract many people who don't feel up to cooking or who dislike eating alone. Where these are not available, neighbors may get together to share cooking chores and have company at mealtime. From earliest childhood, eating is a social activity, and the loss of companionship may destroy appetite, too. Finding someone to share the meal may be all that is needed to make eating pleasurable again.

Those who do not have the strength to prepare meals for themselves, or who are too depressed to try, may be willing to eat if food can be brought to them. Where Meals on Wheels programs exist, they may provide such a solution. Food brought in by family or neighbors or delivered from a restaurant serves the same purpose. Even TV dinners can tempt a flagging appetite and help to maintain nutrition.

Mr. Russell, aged eighty-four, was a resident of a retirement hotel. He was confined to a wheelchair and had never learned to cook. During the week, a retired nurse, who was also a resident of the hotel, came in for a few hours a day to look after him and prepare his meals, but on weekends she visited her children and was not available. Mr. Russell's neighbor across the hall solved the problem by bringing in TV dinners and heating them, thus providing companionship as well as food. Mr. Russell came to prefer the TV dinners to his weekday fare—somewhat to the annoyance of the nurse!

Mr. Russell's experience serves to remind us that food is not only nutrition. It is a means of human contact and a symbol of love, caring, and security. The emotional support provided by the act of bringing food may do more to revive an invalid's interest in life than the food itself. This probably accounts for the fact that many Meals on

Wheels recipients are reluctant to give up the service even when they have become able to obtain their food in other ways. The daily appearance of a caller with the food package means that somebody cares.

The array of physical hazards that old people encounter can be truly formidable, but so is the ingenuity and courage which they often bring to bear in dealing with them. Fortunately, society is now beginning to provide some assistance in overcoming these obstacles and thus improving the quality of life for the elderly. (Appendix III contains help in locating agencies that provide such services.)

Old People Are Not as Fragile as We Think: A Lifetime of Coping

One of the chief obstacles to successful aging is the assumption, prevalent in our culture, that not much can be expected of old people. We forget that those who have lived into their seventies, eighties, and beyond have had a lifetime of coping. They have survived the childhood diseases that ravaged their peers; they have survived wars and depressions; they have known work and marriage and child-rearing, successes and setbacks. Despite increasing physical weakness, the old are not as fragile as we think. If they were, they wouldn't be here. One old lady, hospitalized for a suspected tumor, reminded her anxious son of this fact: "Don't worry, dear, whatever happens, I won't die young."

4

Personality Changes: "Grandma Never Used to Be Like This"

The neighbors of Martha Corning (see page 69) have been worried about her lately. She used to be one of the friendliest people in her building, going out of her way to help others despite her own handicaps. In recent weeks, however, she has been suspicious even of her best friends. She accused one neighbor of "wanting to put her in a nursing home" although the woman had never said anything of the sort, and was, in fact, one of the strongest supporters of Martha's independence. Convinced that she "saw" her divorced and long-dead husband in her apartment at night, Martha had her locks changed, which prevented anyone from coming in to help her when she was ill. Her formerly immaculate apartment became filthy, her plants neglected. She seldom answered the telephone, and when she did, her speech often sounded slurred and incoherent. Her neighbors were at a loss to know what to do. "What can be happening to Martha?" they asked each other. "Is she becoming senile?"

One friend finally took it upon herself to call Martha's doctors and to try to locate her family. After considerable detective work, she was able to get in touch with a niece. Working together, the neighbors, the doctors, and the niece were, in time, able to persuade Martha to enter a hospital. There it was discovered that the culprit was the medication she had been taking. Once "dried out," and re-established on a less toxic regimen, Martha became her old self again.

Even more than physical deterioration, changes in mental functioning are anticipated and feared both by the elderly themselves and by their families. Will Grandma become a forgetful, repetitious, querulous old crone? Will Grandpa lose his good judgment and spend money foolishly, or perhaps become secretive and suspicious? In considering the changes of aging, it is important to distinguish what is normal and self-limiting from that which is pathological and requires treatment and help.

Memory Loss: The Bogey of "Chronic Brain Syndrome"

Senility, medically known as "chronic organic brain syndrome," is the bogey of every aged person. Inability to remember a name "on the tip of my tongue" rouses the latent fear: "What if I get too helpless to manage? What if my mind goes?" Conjured up are nightmare images of institutionalization, being consigned to the indifferent care of strangers, becoming "a vegetable," the vacant mind having been robbed of effective means of redress or control. This central fear of helplessness is expressed succinctly in the Bible (John 21:18): "When thou wast young, thou girdedst thyself, and walkedst whither thou wouldest: but when thou shalt be old, thou shalt stretch forth thy hands, and another shall gird thee, and carry thee whither thou wouldest not."

Small wonder that the reaction to evidence of memory loss is apt to be panic.

Mrs. Brown, eighty-one, was horrified when she discovered that she had mailed a birthday present intended for one grandniece to another grandniece's address. Since the girls were sisters who moved frequently, it was an understandable error, but Mrs. Brown was deeply shaken. She confided her fears to the girls' mother, a very favorite relative. "I don't know how I could have done such a thing— I must be losing my mind. Whatever will become of Harry if anything happens to me. . . . You know how he goes out to get the paper and half the time he forgets to buy it. He put the checkbook away last week and we couldn't find it for hours . . . and Monday he thought it was Tuesday." Harry, her husband, was more philosophical, or perhaps more able to deny that anything could be wrong. "She's all right," he insisted. "Doing better than I am, if you want to know."

Mrs. Brown's anxiety was partly due to growing concern about herself and her awareness that her husband was becoming more forgetful. However, it was also partly due to our cultural habit of ascribing to the effects of aging anything that happens to an old person. If a twenty-six-year-old mislays a book or thinks Monday is Tuesday, no one worries about it.

Memory loss, in most elderly people, remains a mild nuisance and does not become a disability. It should be cause for alarm only if it interferes with self-care or safety. The man who goes for a walk and forgets how to get home and the woman who regularly forgets to turn off the stove and burns the food, and perhaps herself, are obviously in trouble. The cause and treatment of the trouble may not be so obvious. Severe memory loss, confusion, and agitation are often ascribed to hardening of the arteries, without any thorough medical investigation. Unfortunately, although "chronic organic brain syndrome" is a respectable medical diagnosis, it is all too often resorted to as a facile excuse for doing nothing. It is likely to mean that we don't really know what ails the patient, but he's over sixty-five. As a catchall, it rivals "It's a virus," but with far more devastating consequences. The appearance of confusion may mask, among other things, a heart attack or acute diabetes, infection, improper medication, malnutrition, or depression. It is never safe to assume that symptoms of trouble are due to aging and are therefore inaccessible to treatment.

Even when investigation has determined that organic brain damage exists, the severity of the symptoms depends a great deal on how the patient is treated. A psychologist who has done considerable research on "altered brain function" tells a story of how he and his colleagues devised a group of questionnaires and sensory-stimulus tests that would indicate the presence of brain damage. They then looked in the back wards of a state hospital to find a subject on whom to test their findings. They found one old man— unkempt, disheveled, incontinent—staring vacantly at the floor. They were not surprised when all their tests showed "altered brain function." They asked that the man be brought to a seminar that they were conducting the following day, so that they could demonstrate the tests. When the patient appeared, however, he had been washed, shaved, and dressed in street clothes. He seemed surprisingly responsive and alert, interested in what was going on. When the tests were administered, all the results which had been positive the previous day were now negative.

"The difference between a lady and a flower girl," said Eliza Doolittle in Shaw's *Pygmalion*, "is not how she acts but how she is treated." The difference between a human being and a vegetable may well be the same.

Selective Inattention

What appears to be memory loss may also be a device to block out emotional pain, and might be better defined as "selective inattention." Grandfather may be able to remember all the baseball scores of 1928, but forgets that he has a doctor's appointment to check his high blood pressure and those odd pains that have been bothering him lately. This is a phenomenon not unknown to younger people. Who has not had the experience of forgetting an unwelcome task or a dinner invitation from a cantankerous relative? Perhaps old people do take refuge, at times, in the infirmities of age as an excuse for avoiding things they never liked doing anyway. If so, they are not so much different from the rest of us. We all use excuses when it suits us. "I can't bake for the P.T.A.—I'm working full time." "I can't drive your Uncle Jim to the airport on Saturday, that's the annual office golf outing." "I have a headache."

The Myth of Mental Decline

Contrary to popular mythology, there need not be a decline in the ability to think clearly and productively in the later years. A study of healthy people between sixty and seventy-five found no decrease in their I.Q. scores. In occupations where retirement is not mandatory, such as law, medicine, or music, people often continue to be productive as long as they are in good health. Whereas these people are likely to say, "Thank God I still have my health," their younger families are more likely to say, "Thank God Dad still has all his faculties—his mind is clear as a bell!"

Even the ability to engage in new learning does not necessarily decrease in old age, but it takes longer and requires more energy. This is probably why old people are selective about the new tasks they take on, and generally prefer familiar surroundings and activities.

Brain damage, debilitating illness, depression do affect thinking ability, as they would at any age. Probably a more common reason for decrease in brain power is disuse. When people stop learning and growing, they do become less able to think clearly and effectively. As with any other function, "Use it or you lose it." There may be more than casual similarity between the retired executive who seems to have lost the ability to do anything but putter and the housewife who hasn't opened a book since graduation and complains she is stagnating. Perhaps the logical successor to women's liberation is the recovery of meaningful roles for those who have become an obsolete generation. Good physical health in old age depends to a great extent on good health habits of earlier years, and the life of the mind is likewise affected by its use or disuse. Jennie Swerdlow, a sixty-eight-year-old Russian immigrant, expressed this fact succinctly. "It's not exactly what you do when you're past 65," she says. "It's what you did all your life that matters. If you've lived a full life, developed your mind, you'll be able to use it past 65. Let the young people put that in their soup and eat it."[1] Clearly, the time to prepare for old age is in adolescence.

When memory is affected (unless it is "selective inattention"), it is usually recent memory that suffers most, and with it, perhaps, the ability to attend to multitudinous details. Whether this is due to organic change or decrease in available energy would be difficult to establish, and in any case it doesn't matter. When it happens, the wisest course is probably to shift the burden of detail to someone who finds it less onerous. Mr. Belofsky (see pages 16 and 27) resorted to this solution. Despite his years of business experience, at eighty-seven he found himself having trouble balancing his checkbook and keeping records straight. "I've no head for figures anymore," he told his son. "You do it." He then settled back happily to teach his grandson, whom he had earlier prepared for his Bar Mitzvah, the principles of chess. While relinquishing those tasks which were beginning to demand a disproportionate amount of his effort and concentration, he was able to draw on his accumulated knowledge and the joy of a lifetime hobby. Substituting wisdom for energy is one means of accommodating to the loss or decline of function. If the remaining strengths can be utilized, the deficits may not cause so much anguish.

Personality Changes May Be Reactions to Loss

Other personality changes, which are sometimes put down to "hardening of the arteries," may in fact be reactions to stress. The loss of a spouse or other important person, or a decline in physical or mental functioning, may sometimes precipitate bizarre behavior.

Mr. Davis had always depended on his wife to make important decisions. During her final illness, he had a hard time dealing with the fact of her disability and impending death. His task was not made easier by his wife's raging at him with accusations of blame for all her disappointments in their life together, nor by their children's assumption that he was incompetent to deal with her care.

After her death, as he struggled to decide how to spend the rest of his life, he began to exhibit confusion and forgetfulness. He wandered about at night and did not recognize his children or his doctors. He became incontinent, lost interest in food, and talked incoherently about visits from his dead wife. His behavior was ascribed to poor circulation, but after a few weeks the symptoms disappeared almost as suddenly as they had developed. In his case, they had been caused not by organic changes but by an acute grief reaction. Mr. Davis had suffered a special kind of heartbreak with the loss of his wife, and needed the healing of time to put the pain of her last months of life in proper perspective.

Agitation, Anxiety, Complaints, and Demands

A common reaction to loss, either social or physical, may be an increase in the demands on those remaining, whether they be family and caretakers or casual observers such as friends and neighbors.

One old lady, Mrs. Graham, habitually called the police when her daughter was not home to answer the telephone, to the embarrassment of the daughter and the exasperation of the police. As friends dropped away and her health declined, her fear of losing her only surviving child became more desperate. Husband, sons, sister—all were gone. Who now would protect her against a lonely world, or against her own infirmities? No one person, of course, can supply such all-encompassing security, and the daughter felt overwhelmed. However, when a neighborhood center opened near Mrs. Graham's apartment, the old lady began to spend time there regularly. As she met new friends, the frantic telephone calls to her daughter decreased, and the police were no longer summoned. But she complained more about her health, even to her new-found friends. After all, her poor health was still with her, and it felt so good to have someone who would listen to her complaints!

Not all signals for help are as dramatic as a call to the police department. Many people just talk about their aches and pains. There is often a realistic basis for these, but underlying the physical discomfort may be the emotional ache of loneliness, boredom, fear, or feeling superfluous.

Mrs. Marshall, aged seventy-eight, had lived for ten years with her daughter and son-in-law after the death of her husband. As grandchildren left home, the younger couple planned a move to smaller quarters. Mrs. Marshall moved into a low-rent building for senior citizens. Not long afterward, she called a community agency serving the elderly and asked if they could send someone to "give a massage." It seemed a peculiar request, but Mrs. Marshall explained it to the social worker who visited. She had arthritis in her back, and her husband used to massage her to relieve the pain. After his death, her daughter continued this practice. Now that she was alone, she had no one to rub her back. Furthermore, she didn't even have a tub in her new apartment, only a shower. How could anyone get really comfortable in a shower? In addition to describing her discomfort, Mrs. Marshall overwhelmed her young visitor with questions and compliments: "Such a pretty girl! Do you have a boyfriend? What a pity I'm not able to introduce you to my grandson—a lovely girl like you should be married." The emotional hunger clearly outweighed the physical pain.

Mrs. Marshall eventually solved her massage problem by installing a special shower head, and making twice-weekly visits to the daughter's home where she could enjoy both a hot tub and the warmth of a relationship. But she really gained a new lease on life when her sister broke her arm. Now, once more, somebody really needed her, and the arthritic pain receded in importance.

An increase in physical symptoms at times of emotional

stress is not the sole prerogative of the elderly. People of all ages exhibit the phenomenon, from "examination headaches" to executive ulcers. In a residential home for children, some years ago, the children lived in large dormitories with housemothers who worked eight-hour shifts. The home had a large and heavily used infirmary, with two full-time nurses. When the dormitory groups were reduced in size and the succession of three-shift workers was replaced by live-in housemothers, the use of the infirmary fell off so dramatically that it was reduced to two beds for children suffering from contagious illnesses or other emergencies, with one nurse in attendance. The children no longer needed to get their "tender loving care" from the nurses when they could get it from their now more available houseparents.

Those who exhibit agitation, complaints, or constant demands for attention can often be helped if more human contact and significant activity can be built into their lives. Providing more services may not be the best solution, even when the services are available. For instance, Greta Ulschuler, a formerly vigorous, outgoing lady in her seventies, became a whining, complaining "nudge" after her husband died and a chronic heart problem required her to restrict her activities. She called every agency in town asking for help. Although her daughter shopped for her every day, she also wanted cooked meals delivered, a nurse to give her a bath, a housekeeper to clean the apartment that she had always kept immaculate by herself. The more she got, the more depressed and disabled she seemed to become. Many days she did not even get dressed, but sat all day in a housecoat, her hair uncombed. When the agency that had been providing the meals stopped them, and offered instead an opportunity to spend a week at a camp for senior citizens, she complained bitterly, but finally agreed to go. She had a wonderful time, and those who knew her as "poor old sick Mrs. Ulschuler" would not have believed their eyes if they saw her at camp. Later, she joined the local chapter of Seniors Alert, an organization concerned with legislation affecting the elderly, and before long she was its recording secretary. The energy that had gone into arguing about meals and maid service was channeled into working for more adequate resources for all elderly people. She regained so much of her old spirit that when her granddaughter's first baby was born, the granddaughter asked Mrs. Ulschuler to come and spend a week with her to help out. Mrs. Ulschuler was delighted. Her demands for assistance had not really been the result of poor health, but rather an effort to substitute *something* for the relationships and functions she had lost. Offered a more adequate substitute, she was able to make good use of it.

Those who resort to complaints, demands, and general crankiness may not actually be exhibiting a personality change so much as an intensification of an earlier pattern. Mrs. Ulschuler, for instance, had always been outspoken, and Mrs. Graham, the lady who called the police, had always been rather fluttery and anxious. When aging multiplied their losses and decreased their options, the pattern became more noticeable. Yet for each it served the same purpose as before—to prevent isolation, to be in touch with the world, to get one's needs met. "The squeaking wheel gets the oil," and those who have learned to "squeak" early in life may be better prepared to cope with the hazards of aging than those who are more passive.

Most fortunate of all, of course, are those who have learned to cope by charm, and keep the ability in old age. To be able to get people to want to do things for you is the most useful of social skills. Mr. Martin, an old gentleman who lives alone in a rural area, is confined to a wheelchair because of a back injury. However, his big lawn is always beautifully cut. The neighborhood children vie with each other for the privilege of cutting Mr. Martin's grass because he has a knack of making them feel ten feet tall. For these fortunate souls, locked doors swing open at a touch, and the service delivery system that creaks and groans for others glides smoothly and efficiently. Blessed are the charmers, for they not only get what they need but their helpers feel lucky to know them!

Denial, Poor Judgment, and Rejection of Help

Instead of demanding help, some people react to the disabilities of aging by refusing to admit that anything is wrong, or that changes or help of any kind may be needed. Someone in obvious need of clothing, food, or assistance may refuse to spend any money for these purposes, even though the resources are available. They persist in saving "for a rainy day" when it is already pouring. In so doing, they try to fend off the awareness of deterioration and the encroachments of time. Others may deny the realities of a decreased income by continuing to maintain aspects of a life style that they can no longer afford, like the lady who skimps on food and needed medical care, but never skips her weekly appointment at the beauty parlor. That ritual is her flag of defiance, her reminder to herself and the world that she is still somebody. Denial is also the coping method used by those who persist in doing tasks beyond their strength, who refuse to see a doctor or accept any help. Perhaps they fear that if they ever admitted the magnitude of the odds against them, they would be swept away. Their

affirmation of life is to continue to do the impossible, or
at least the unnecessary.

Some degree of denial is useful in that it enables people
to carry on independently longer than they might have
otherwise been able to do. "Pop," the seventy-seven-year-
old fisherman (see page 75), certainly maintained his mobility longer by ignoring his discomforts. Carried to an extreme, however, denial may accelerate the very process
it was intended to prevent. If Grandma defies dizziness
by climbing on a chair to get the drapes down, she may
very well fall off and break a hip.

It is just such possibilities that worry families who see
their elders showing "poor judgment" by refusing to recognize change or accept help. Sometimes the stubborn one
can be persuaded to accept a *little* help, and when he or
she sees that the world has not come to an end after all,
a little more may be accepted.

Sarah Goldfarb drove her family to distraction because,
despite failing memory and poor eyesight, she refused all
their efforts to provide help. Her apartment was a mess,
her clothes dirty and ragged, her hair an untidy mop. New
clothes hung in the closet unused because they were "too
nice to wear." Food brought in might go uneaten because
she could not remember where she had put it. Her daughter
wanted to move her out bodily and clean everything at
once, but was persuaded to try a more gradual approach.
A young girl named Susan who lived in the building visited
Mrs. Goldfarb, made friends with her, and accepted the
old lady's offer of tea and cookies. Before long, it seemed
natural for Susan to carry the teapot to the table, and to
help with the dishes afterward. Little by little, she was allowed to do more—sweep the floor, take out the garbage,
even defrost the refrigerator. In nice weather, Mrs. Goldfarb began to go for walks with her young friend, and finally

agreed to accompany her to the beauty parlor. Both had their hair washed and set. Mrs. Goldfarb's had to be cut short before anything could be done with it, so tangled had it become. She was reluctant to permit the haircut, but finally submitted because Susan was having hers done, too. She was quite pleased with the result, and became more willing to wear her new clothes and to accompany her daughter's family to a restaurant. Finally, she even agreed to having hot meals sent in several times a week, if Susan would eat with her.

Mrs. Goldfarb's story illustrates how even confused people, who are trying desperately to deny their disabilities, may be enabled to use help if they can develop a relationship of confidence with their helpers. This is a process which requires much patience and time, but it is well worth the effort.

Inconsistency

Some people combine demands for and refusals of help in a fashion that is both confusing and exasperating to their families and would-be helpers. One sixty-five-year-old woman, Mrs. Peasgood, called her local area office on aging to complain that she had not been able to get any household help—none of the agencies that were supposed to provide such service would give it to her. Why were they discriminating against her? When an agency worker called her to plan for service, however, she could not agree to an appointment: 10 A.M. was too early—her niece was coming at eleven; twelve was too late; Tuesday she had to see the doctor. Something was wrong with every day and time that was offered. When the worker suggested that perhaps Mrs. Peasgood was not really in need of service, she replied angrily, "I don't see why you keep pestering me. You people never do anything anyhow!" Mr. Sanger, an eighty-five-year-old man severely disabled by a variety of illnesses, had to depend on a number of services to remain in his apartment. Meals on Wheels were delivered daily, a housekeeper cleaned his apartment every week, and a home health aide came twice a week to give him a bath, do his laundry, and take care of other errands. Mr. Sanger accepted these services, but with a snarl. He complained constantly about their inadequacy. The housekeeper was late—the meals were cold—the shopper brought him chicken legs attached to the thighs when he wanted them disjointed. It was all a conspiracy to defraud and humiliate the elderly, he insisted, and usually wound up his diatribe by asserting, "There was better food in the concentration camps!" As a result, keeping services available to Mr. Sanger became a job in itself. Housekeepers quit in tears, volunteers refused to deliver meals, the shopper asked to be assigned to somebody else. And Mr. Sanger would conclude, almost triumphantly, "You see, nobody wants to help a poor old man!"

Such behavior is often ascribed to confusion and senility, but it is more likely to be the result of rage. Mrs. Peasgood, Mr. Sanger, and others like them are so infuriated by the increasing weakness that requires them to seek help that they lash out at their helpers. Their unrealistic demands are an effort to regain a sense of control of their lives. Sometimes, if they can be helped to recognize the anger, they can learn more acceptable ways of expressing it, and thus stop sabotaging the services they need.

Suspiciousness and Unfounded Accusations

In all instances where there is a tendency to deny the deficits brought by aging, the central issue is one of the older person's need to maintain control over his life and circumstances. One of the most bewildering attempts to maintain control is the reaction of the person who tries to fend off memory loss and other failing faculties by casting accusations at others. When Mrs. Barnett cannot remember where she put her stockings, she may accuse her daughter or her neighbor of stealing them. Mrs. Jameson, a stroke victim, enraged at having to sit passively while a house-keeper performed what used to be her chores, accused the woman of stealing her pots and pans. Efforts to prove that nothing was missing were to no avail. Mrs. Jameson insisted that she wouldn't have a thief in her house and discharged the housekeeper. In a sense, the housekeeper *was* stealing from Mrs. Jameson—stealing her role as a homemaker. Mrs. Jameson had to be moved to a nursing home. She did not like it, but at least she did not have to suffer the indignity of watching another woman usurp her domain.

Other forms of unreasonable suspiciousness are some-times adopted by isolated and lonely people. One such woman developed a conviction that she was the chosen victim of a conspiracy to rob and murder the elderly. When regular visits from a friend enabled her to discuss her fears about her worsening health and her alienation from her family, the conspiracy theme disappeared from her conver-sation. An isolated man nearly suffered eviction because of his habit of banging his cane on the ceiling in the middle of the night. He was convinced that his neighbors were deliberately making noise in order to harass and frighten him. He was too wary to accept help to refocus the problem, sensing intuitively that perhaps the problem was his. When his family arranged for a daily delivery of meals to him, the brief contacts with the volunteer who brought them seemed to calm his overall anxiety. He did not become less paranoid in his thinking, but he did desist from knocking on the ceiling.

The most generally successful method of dealing with paranoid behavior in the elderly is to increase the amount of contact and attention they receive. However, this must be done with caution, because such people are limited in their ability to engage in personal relationships, and are easily threatened by too much closeness. Determining how much contact is helpful to such a person, like determining how much insulin is needed by a diabetic, must be done on an individual basis. The patient's response is the only reliable guide.

Withdrawal, Apathy, Depression, and Mourning

Agitation, angry demands, and suspiciousness, while often difficult to live with, are all active responses to loss. Other people respond more passively, by "flight" rather than "fight." The woman who gives up her bridge games and seldom leaves the house and the man who immerses himself in the newspaper (sometimes dozing behind it) instead of seeking out his cronies may cause concern to their families. "Mother should get out more," they say. "Father just sits like a bump on a log. We should help him to find an interest in life."

Actually, the apparent disengagement may be a strategic retreat, necessary for the conservation of energy for those activities which still hold interest and importance. One great-grandmother, well beyond her hundredth birthday, delighted in family parties. She turned herself out in great style and was the star of each occasion, for about half an hour. Then she would sit contentedly listening to the conversations going on around her—she was nearly blind—and responding to those who stopped to chat with her. Afterward she would go to bed for a week. It would have been a shame if the family had curtailed her participation because it was "too tiring for her," for those parties were what she lived for.

Disengagement and apparent apathy may also serve to insulate the person from emotional pain. To continue with one's accustomed social activities when fingers are clumsy or speech is slurred may be an embarrassment rather than a pleasure, a painful reminder of loss and deterioration. Mr. Rogers, who had been very active in the chamber of commerce and on the town library board, suffered a stroke when he was in his early sixties. Although he made considerable physical recovery, he never became reconciled to the fact that his functioning was permanently impaired. He avoided old friends and all reminders of his previous successes. When it appeared that he would never be able to walk without the aid of a walker or four-pronged cane he gave up walking at all. He preferred to spend his days in bed, his ears stuffed with cotton and a black cloth over his eyes—literally shutting out the world. His reaction was an extreme one, but many who do not go to such lengths manage their feelings by tuning out painful realities. Not all old people are Margaret McClendons (see page 53) any more than all young people are Johnny Gunthers (see page 55). Some, in any age category, prefer to "take their marbles and go home." Of course, if the withdrawal becomes so extreme that the individual neglects to eat or care for himself, his family or associates may have to take active measures to provide what is necessary, or make plans to arrange for institutional care.

Whatever the individual's style of coping with the aging process, it probably reflects his style of coping with the stresses of earlier years. There is truth in the saying that old people are as they always were, only more so. This does not mean that old people cannot learn or change. They can and do. But, generally speaking, apples do not become oranges.

Mourning As a Bridge Between Life Styles

Sometimes the apparent withdrawal of an elderly person is part of a mourning process. Many people do not recognize mourning as an essential part of coping with loss, whether the loss is that of a relationship, a function, or some other part of one's life. All too often, well-meaning friends or relatives see mourning as a problem to be circumvented, rather than as a necessary bridge from one phase of life to another. They may rush to get Mother out of the house where the memories are, "so she won't have to brood over Dad." But brooding may be exactly what she has to do in order to consolidate the memories of her life with him before moving into the next experience. ("Broody" originally referred to a hen sitting on eggs; a "brooding" person may also be hatching something.)

Mourning for a person is generally recognized as such, if not always honored. What is not so generally recognized is the need to mourn for other losses. The man who has gone from affluence to Social Security, the woman who can no longer see well enough to drive, the former history teacher who can't remember dates are also bereaved. They have lost a function, a piece of their independence, an element of their self-image. Younger family members may be puzzled when their offers of help do not stop the complaints. "Why is Dad making such a fuss?" they may ask. "We told him we'd help with the rent—we each give him a check every month—but he still worries about how he's going to manage." They may not recognize that Dad is grieving for the loss of his ability to meet all his own expenses and provide for his children, rather than having to depend on them to provide for him. Children may also not recognize their own mourning over the deterioration of a parent. "Don't make such a fuss" may be a plea to the parent not to confront them with painful reminders that he will not always be around. For them, too, mourning is a means of coping with loss or anticipated loss. If they recognize what is happening, the different generations can reinforce, rather than interfere with, each other's coping styles.

An aspect of mourning that sometimes worries families is that one loss stirs up memories of others. The new widow may talk not only about her husband's death, but also about her mother's. Someone confronted with a disabling illness may dwell on the death of a childhood friend or a career disappointment. To observers, this could be seen as evidence of severe depression, but in fact it is more likely to be a means of integrating earlier life experiences, and therefore a healthy experience.

Depression: Life Stance or Reaction to Loss

The normal reaction to loss is grief. When grief is prolonged, perhaps by a series of losses, or when it is suppressed and unresolved, it may become depression. It is easy to understand gloomy feelings when things are going badly and no respite is in sight. However, it is assumed that depressed feelings in reaction to specific losses will usually clear up as the grief is expressed, worked through, and healed by time.

The depression that is harder to live with is one that

persists even when external circumstances do not warrant it; when, despite the sunshine outside, one's internal climate remains dull gray and overcast. When that happens, happy occasions give no pleasure, food loses its taste and sleep its consolation, and a sense of worthlessness and hopelessness pervades the mind and prevents enjoyment of both one's own company and the company of others. No accomplishment seems valid, no effort worthwhile. To those struggling in this depth of despondency, it may require all the determination they can muster just to get up in the morning. It is one of the most painful and debilitating of all illnesses, the more so because, by its nature, it saps the will to contend against it. Entreaties by well-meaning family to "snap out of it" and "cheer up" only serve to deepen the sense of all-pervasive aloneness with the terrible burden and reinforce the powerlessness to deal with it. Depression of this magnitude is a treatable illness and requires psychiatric care as surely as severe diabetes requires medical care.

Between normal grief reactions and acute depressive episodes are the chronic depressions that may have been lifelong. Those whose self-esteem has always been fragile, perhaps totally dependent on some form of validation such as work, or looks, or the maternal role, may be devastated when that support is removed. Recovery from a particular loss does not seem to depend on the nature of the loss itself so much as on the degree of self-worth that was bound up with it and on how many other resources remain available.

Repetition, Reminiscence, and Life Review

Increased repetitiveness is a behavior change that is often considered proof of senility. Repeating the same question over and over is indeed sometimes a means of coping with memory loss—a way to remind oneself of who and where one is. It may also be an effort to remind others of one's existence and needs. The old man who asks again and again what time his son is coming to take him to the doctor may be less concerned about time than about reassurance that someone will really come. A busy housewife commented to a visitor that her mother had repeated six times that morning that the tulips would soon be in bloom. "Well," said the visitor, "did anybody answer her?" Nobody had.

Old people often like to talk about the past, and younger listeners may find these recollections boring and repetitious. Preoccupation with the past is often considered evidence of inability to deal with the present, especially when it increases at times of current crisis. Observers are, therefore, likely to ignore references to the past, or to try to bring the old person "back to reality" by refocusing his attention on the present situation.

However, the buried memories that surface with a new stress or loss may provide a unique opportunity for resolving old conflicts and thus strengthening the elderly (or not so elderly) person's powers of coping with current reality. Going over the old ground with an interested listener can provide a means for the integration of unfinished business— the loose ends, the failures, the disappointments that come back to haunt one in the middle of the night.

Amy Openshaw was ninety-five and terminally ill. Her husband had died many years earlier and she had no close relatives. One might have supposed that Mrs. Openshaw would have no energy to concern herself with the past, that her current needs for comfort and care would be her only preoccupation. Yet the social worker who was called in to help with practical matters found herself listening, instead, to Mrs. Openshaw's troubled memory of her husband's illness and death twenty years earlier. Had she taken good enough care of him? Oh, she had nursed him well, no doubt of that, but had she really cared enough? She remembered resentment, impatience, weariness. The story shifted to a youthful, unfulfilled romance. The young man had married someone else, and when Amy eventually married, she found her husband disappointing in many ways. Perhaps she had never loved him as a wife should. No, she had never been physically unfaithful, but she was haunted by the Biblical warning that one who "looks lustfully" at another has already "committed adultery in his heart." She had never forgotten her youthful lover; was she guilty of unfaithfulness after all?

The worker listened and did not judge or censure. Mrs. Openshaw had to go over the story several times before she was able to conclude that although she had had an ungratifying marriage, she need not feel guilty about her role in it. She was also able to acknowledge that she had never felt free to share the story with anyone before, but that the combination of increased need and a willing listener enabled her to do so now. Thus unburdened, she was able to address herself to the here-and-now. She seemed much more content, and began to speak with philosophical acceptance of her approaching death. It appeared that she could neither use her remaining energy for living nor die in peace until she had been enabled to forgive herself for that old and festering "failure."

It is not only the dark and tormenting secrets that can be exorcised by reminiscence with a receptive audience. Successes that have been pushed into the background by current losses may be relived and enjoyed. The recognition of what one's life has consisted of, what and who has mattered and still matters, how one has contributed to the future of his family or community—all these can enhance one's sense of inner integrity, of not having lived in vain. The positives that have been salvaged can be enumerated, thus helping to put the disappointments in perspective. The drawing up of such an accounting can lead to a sense of accomplishment, as well as clearing the slate before the final reckoning.

Reminiscence serves the additional purpose of conveying the value of one's life to others. It is particularly valuable when the listeners are members of one's own family, those who will remember and whose own sense of continuity may be strengthened by this contact with their roots. A group worker who made tape recordings of the recollections of elderly immigrants was asked by one of the participants, a ninety-two-year-old man, if he could have a copy of the tape. "I'd like to leave it to my grandchildren," he said. In this instance the legacy was a double one, for the original went into an oral-history collection as part of the archives of "The Jewish Experience in America," exhibited in the Chicago Museum of Science and Industry in 1976. Thus it will help to give not only the man's own grandchildren but many other children a sense of rootedness and continuity. Reminiscence looks backward in order to go forward with the generations yet to come.

The person who is engaged in reminiscence may present himself very differently when he is describing his ailments and needs. Greta Ulschuler, whom we met earlier, talked at great length about her heart palpitations, her shortness of breath, and her inadequate Social Security when she was making a case for home-delivered meals or a rent subsidy. Yet when a volunteer came to interview her about her early experiences in this country, as part of an oral-history project, he heard a story full of humorous recollections of ingenious coping with an immigrant's lot. There was no mention of sickness or poverty except as obstacles that had been successfully overcome. Reminiscence, by emphasizing strengths instead of deficits, can help to restore self-esteem. This can, in turn, make it more palatable for the older person to accept help when it is needed. The focus is, after all, not on total dysfunction, but only on needs that exist in certain areas.

The Many Faces of Aging: Game-Playing or Survival Technique?

The different faces shown in various situations by elderly people are sometimes seen as evidences of manipulation or playacting. Yet we all present ourselves differently to different audiences. Consider, for example, the young housewife who is bragging to the neighbors about her husband's raise; how her view of their economic situation changes when she contemplates their income-tax return!

Such varying behavior may provide an ingenious means of dealing with uncomfortable situations. A man who moved into a housing project for the elderly found that most of his new neighbors were very different from him in background and education. He found many of them uncongenial, but did not want to hurt their feelings. Therefore, whenever he was visited by people who bored him, he was "too sick" for company. Yet when old or new friends dropped in to play chess or share library books, he made a miraculous recovery. A psychologist might label this as devious behavior, but any hostess would recognize it as a valuable technique for social survival. This again illustrates our cultural tendency to censure in old people some behavior that we condone or even admire in young ones.

It might be helpful to remember that most of the behaviors seen as shifts in personality in the elderly are the result of efforts to cope with the social, physical, and psychological changes encountered in the aging process. Reviewing some of the coping strategies and life styles adopted by old people, we see how infinite are human variety and inventiveness. Those who have not yet achieved old age may find this reassuring, both as they observe the adaptations old people make and as they contemplate that they are getting older themselves.

The Expanding Self

Personality change in old age is usually assumed to be change for the worse, the result of loss of function. Perhaps because they do not create a problem, we forget the changes that result from increased wisdom, compassion, or breadth of vision. Not having to worry about keeping a job or getting a promotion may bring a freedom of action unavailable to younger people. It has been noted that two major political upsets—Watergate and the Army-McCarthy hearings— were achieved not by young upstarts but by old lawyers. A similar, though less spectacular phenomenon is often observed within families. Grandpa, regardless of his strictness with his own sons, may become the confidant of his grandsons and encourage their special desires and ambitions.

The mellowing of age is not entirely a myth. A college girl, making a duty visit to her great-aunt, was surprised to discover that the old lady, whom she remembered as a rather strict and nervous disciplinarian, had become a detached and humorous observer of the social scene, and a spellbinding storyteller. Perhaps the relinquishment of responsibility had given her a chance to develop this aspect of her personality. The cleverness had always been there, but what had earlier been presented as abruptness and sarcasm was now gentler and more tolerant.

Dorothy Canfield Fisher, in one of her short stories, condenses the process of gaining wisdom into three episodes. A woman recalls an incident of her teen years, and retells it three times—once in her thirties, again in her fifties, and finally in her eighties. In each telling, she reveals an expansion of the meaning of the event, and an increase in her own common sense, wisdom, and compassion.[2] Such increments to selfhood are more common than we realize. Perhaps because of our tendency to focus on problems, and to limit our expectations of growth to the younger years, we do not always recognize still-developing potential when we see it. Douglas Steere credits a seventeenth-century writer with this perceptive view of the human condition: "It was a wonderful thing to recognize the advanced age of a person, less by the infirmity of his body than by the maturity of his soul."[3]

Personality changes, whether coping strategies for dealing with loss or expansion of selfhood through new roles and attitudes, are testimony to human flexibility, inventiveness, and capacity for growth. As such, they may be reassuring to those who have not yet achieved old age!

5

The Middle Generation: Beset from Both Sides

The Mid-Life Crisis

While the oldest generation is coping with the demanding tasks of aging, their children, the middle generation, are facing a set of problems that are different, yet in some ways similar. It is the middle-aged who must deal with both the adulthood of their children and the decline of their parents, and, in so doing, discover and judge their own individuality. Just as the young question, by words or behavior, the values of their elders, their parents' half-suppressed doubts may emerge in a painful reassessment: "What kind of parent have I been? What have I accomplished? What has my life been worth?" And as the parents' own parents become physically weaker and perhaps more dependent, they, too, serve as a reminder that time is not infinite.

It is during the middle years that the divorce rate soars, careers are changed or newly begun, and books and plays are written. It is not the young who feel constrained, as Robert Herrick advised, to "gather ye rosebuds while ye may" but the middle-aged. A study of terminally ill patients indicated that those aged forty to fifty-five fear death more than those older or younger.[1] This is probably related to the mid-life sense of having to accomplish or change a great deal in a limited time.

Gail Sheehy describes the passage from "mid-life" to "middleage" as a shift from intense concern with self-image, achievement, and satisfaction or dissatisfaction with existing relationships to a greater degree of self-acceptance and autonomy.[2] Although the dates vary with individuals, the years between forty and sixty are usually seen as a time when people are likely to be in a process of redetermining who they are and of establishing a new balance.

A Conflict Between Self-Realization and Responsibility

A society in the process of rapid change offers many possibilities for personal growth and fulfillment, but these may conflict with family obligations. A woman who is trying to develop a post-child-rearing career may find herself worrying about its effects not only on her husband but on her parents as well. Who will drive Grandpa to the doctor, now that his arthritis keeps him from taking the bus?

Mrs. Cory worries about her father. He doesn't see his friends much anymore. At seventy-seven, he no longer feels up to walking half a mile to the bus and climbing aboard. So he calls a cab, or since cabs are expensive on a Social Security income, he waits for his daughter to take him. But his daughter, who was at home while her children were little, is now working full time, and frequently he loses out to a grandchild. He doesn't complain—much—but Mrs. Cory worries. "I never thought of this ten years ago, or even five," she says pensively.

Perhaps a car pool would help to solve the problem for both Mrs. Cory and her father. Some cities have communal transportation available to the elderly and more is being developed.

Old people are living longer than they used to, while young people are likely to continue their education much longer than their parents did. The responsible generation, the middle-aged, may find itself supporting one or several young adults in college while coping with the health problems of aging parents. How is one to balance the college daughter's wardrobe against Grandma's new dentures? Not only is the financial pressure heavy, but those caught in the squeeze between youngsters and oldsters may feel cheated and resentful. Expected to provide for everybody, when will their own chance for living come?

Mrs. Inman had lived with her daughter's family for twenty years. She was nearly eighty when her oldest grandchild went off to college. Her daughter Virginia drew a long breath, decided it was high time she had a life of her own, and learned to drive. Independently mobile for the first time, she began to spend many hours away from home. Mrs. Inman, used to constant companionship, felt lonely and depressed. Her own mobility was decreasing and her hearing was bad. She brooded and began to feel she was in the way. One night she took an overdose of sleeping pills—not enough to kill her, but enough to scare the family badly. Virginia was not only shocked, but bitter. Must she give up her newly acquired freedom? Was she always to have an albatross around her neck?

At the hospital where Mrs. Inman was treated, the family talked with a social worker about what had happened. Not only did they gain a clearer understanding of the shifts in their family and how these had affected Mrs. Inman's behavior, but they also learned of community resources that might help them in dealing with the changes. A community center within driving distance provided a place where Mrs. Inman could meet and join in activities with people of her own age. She was dubious at first. It was a strange place, and what if Virginia forgot to pick her up? But she was persuaded to try, and as the center became part of her routine she began to enjoy it. When she was no longer exclusively dependent on the family for her social needs, she and her children and grandchildren could once more enjoy each other as people.

Career Versus Caretaker Roles

Establishing a new balance for women often means the beginning or resumption of a career. Children are in school or leaving home, and Mother is at last free to try her own wings. If, at this point, her parents or her husband's parents begin to need more care and attention, she may feel obligated to abandon her own plans and resume a care-giving role. If she does, she will resent it, and if she doesn't, she will probably feel neglectful and guilty. Her problem may be compounded by the fact that the care of elderly relatives, like writing letters and remembering birthdates, is a responsibility often delegated to wives. The aging of parents affects sons as well as daughters, as we shall see, but the decision as to whether and how to change a life style is more likely to affect the son's wife.

A letter from one such wife describes the dilemma vividly. The Andersons had moved from their long-time residence in Pittsburgh when Jim Anderson was transferred to Kansas City. They took Mr. Anderson's eighty-year-old mother with them because she was in uncertain health and had no other children. They settled in a pleasant suburb, and since there were several hospitals within commuting distance, Mary Anderson was able to resume her own career as a consulting dietitian. When the youngest son went away to college, the big house was empty all day. The elder Mrs. Anderson didn't like this at all. She didn't know anybody and had no means of getting acquainted. Since there was no public transportation, activities which might have interested her were inaccessible. She missed her familiar neighborhood in Pittsburgh, her old friends, and her weekly mah-jongg games. She began to complain bitterly about her isolation. "Mary doesn't need to work," she said. "Jim makes a good salary. She could perfectly well stay home and keep me company. When I was young, I certainly didn't leave my mother-in-law to sit and stare at the wall. I don't know what Jim can be thinking of, to let her do it." Mary didn't see it that way. "I'd go stir-crazy, shut up in that house all day. Besides, with two in college, I really do need to work."

The Andersons eventually solved their problem by having Jim's mother enter a home for the aged in Pittsburgh where she could participate in social activities and maintain her ties with old friends. None of them were entirely happy with the solution. Mrs. Anderson felt let down, despite her pleasure in seeing her friends again, and Jim and Mary felt guilty in their relief at being able to continue their own lives. They also experienced some resentment toward each other. Jim felt that Mary might have extended herself more: "After all, how long would it be?" Mary felt denigrated. "I've spent enough of my life with P.T.A. and Little League—I don't want to spend the rest of it talking about mah-jongg. You didn't give up your job here because your mother wanted to live in Pittsburgh, did you? Don't you think my time is worth something?" Yet inwardly she wondered if she had let them down. Mary and Jim suspected that things would have been different if Mrs. Anderson had been Mary's mother instead of Jim's. As the folk saying goes:

> A son's a son till he takes a wife,
> But a daughter's a daughter all her life.

However, there are as many daughters as daughters-in-law who try to juggle the demands of family and job, and still try to get some of their own needs met.

The Expectation Gap

As the Anderson story illustrates, one of the difficulties confronting those in middle life is that their parents' expectations of them are likely to be quite different from their expectations of themselves, and even more different from those of their children. This is particularly true of parents who were immigrants, who probably spent their lives in breadwinner and caretaker roles. Their experience of family life in Europe was that the old were cared for at home, and that there was always at least one woman at home to do it. Now, with more and more women working outside the home, or taking on activities to satisfy their needs rather than other people's, that expectation is not as likely to be filled. It is not that modern families lack concern, or fail to provide emotional and financial support, but that "the woman of the house" does not plan to spend her entire life as a caretaker, focusing only on the needs of others. This change is often very difficult for the older generation to accept—perhaps even more difficult than it is for the middle-aged to accept the different life styles of the young. Trying to reconcile their parents' expectations and their own can lay a heavy burden of guilt on the middle generation.

Old Rules Versus New Self-Images

Even when there is no need for caretaking, the parents' presence and/or expectations may stir up discomfort in both generations, in ways they did not anticipate. The younger ones may feel pressure to resume a role or a way of behaving that they have struggled to outgrow.

When Mr. Fox died, Mrs. Fox's only daughter, Sally, and her husband, Fred, invited her to move in with them. Sally had some misgivings about the arrangement, but Fred insisted that living with them would be a financial saving for Mrs. Fox as well as a help with the children. However, it didn't work out that way. Mrs. Fox disliked late hours, loud radios, and spicy food. Her religiosity clashed with Fred's light-hearted agnosticism. Fred began to feel that his house was no longer his own. He was frequently sulky and abrupt with his mother-in-law, but was careful to say nothing to Sally. Mrs. Fox, feeling less than welcome, spent more and more time in her room. Sally felt guilty about her mother's withdrawal and embarrassed by her husband's rudeness. When, one evening, Fred switched the TV channel in the middle of a program that Mrs. Fox was watching, she did not protest, but Sally did. Fred exploded: "Can't a man watch TV in his own house? Besides, she's *your* mother!" Sally reminded him that inviting Mrs. Fox had been his idea, not hers, and Fred stalked out of the house.

Tramping the streets, Fred could not erase the mental picture of Mrs. Fox retreating to her room and Sally's reproachful silence. Strange, he had never realized how much like her mother Sally was. He felt betrayed. He thought of his own parents—his mother, subservient, busy meeting everyone's needs but her own; his father, autocratic, ignoring everyone's opinion but his own. How eager he had been to get out of that household! He and Sally had thought they were starting something new, free from old patterns. Yet here they were, stuck with the older generation—worse yet, acting like them. Was there no escaping from parents?

A certain amount of privacy and distance is needed if each generation is to fulfill its own needs and realize its own life style. As we are discovering about parent-adolescent coexistence, about marriage, and in fact about most relationships, it is essential to have some distance and privacy even among those who are closest. How much space is required is an individual matter. For Fred, Sally, and Mrs. Fox, life became much easier when Mrs. Fox took a small apartment a few blocks away. The younger family felt free to pursue its own life style, and Mrs. Fox, while enjoying frequent visits, could also enjoy undisturbed sleep, and feel herself once more mistress of her own house rather than an intruder in someone else's.

Reactions to Parental Change: Anxiety, Guilt, Anger

It is one thing to work out a revision of one's expectations of oneself and one's parents while they are functioning independently. But what happens when illness or some other event brings about a drastic change in the parents' abilities? In the ecology of relationships, as in nature, a change in one creates changes in all the others, and with change comes anxiety. This is true regardless of the actual increase in need for care or additional responsibility. Moreover, it is not only the external situation that makes the aging of parents difficult for their children. While those in the middle years are reassessing their accomplishments as adults, the increasing needs of their elderly parents may reawaken the feelings of childhood. For instance, a forty-year-old woman with children of her own and career responsibilities may be astonished to find herself as frightened by her mother's sudden illness as she would have been at ten. In her anxiety she may harass the doctor's secretary many times a day, find fault with everything the nurses do, or berate her own children over trivial mishaps. She may harbor a gnawing sense that she could and should have prevented the catastrophe: that Mother would now be O.K. if only daughter had visited last week instead of entertaining friends, or talked her out of going to the azalea exhibition on a rainy day. Most surprising of all, she may be snappish and irritable with the patient herself. One daughter, more in touch with her feelings than most of us, described her reactions to her mother's stroke: "I know it's a terrible thing to say, but I'm actually *angry* when I see her like that. My mother—always so capable, in charge of everything—now she can't even boil water. I feel like screaming, *"How can you do this to me?"* " Her anger was not so much at having to assume an additional, unanticipated responsibility as it was at the loss of her mother's "motherliness." When a parent can no longer be parental, children of any age feel let down. If they can identify the reason for their anger and disappointment, however, the feelings will be less overwhelming and frightening. The loss can be recognized as real, but not total. It's not the end of the world, even though it may be the beginning of the end of an era.

This is distressing enough when both generations had been leading their own lives. It is devastating when the adult child has depended on the older parent. In many cases, for instance, the older generation is, in fact, an essential part of the family support system. Grandmother may be staying with the grandchildren so that both of their parents can work. As the divorce rate soars, many young mothers move back home as a solution to reduced income and the need for regular and responsible child care. In such households, if Grandpa has a heart attack or Grandma breaks a hip, it means not only that they require care themselves but that the care they provided must be replaced. The family reorganization that results from such a disaster affects the lives not only of the old people but also of the children and grandchildren even unto the third and fourth generation. American family mythology is apt to blind us to this fact of life. Despite all the evidence to the contrary, we tend to suppose that, except for a few unfortunate exceptions, all families consist of two parents, that mother stays home with the children, and that old people, if they exist, are dependent and useless. We believe this in spite of our own experiences and those of our friends—a prime example of the triumph of myth over reason!

The child who must reorganize his or her own support system in addition to providing care for an ailing parent has indeed a heavy burden. But even if the parent has not been providing any actual services, his or her existence as a functioning adult supports the feeling that everything is O.K., that one is not alone, that there is still time. Signs of disability in a parent suddenly serve as a reminder that this will not always be so. As the birth of one's first baby marks the change in a young adult's role from that of a child to that of an adult, so the loss, or anticipated loss, of a parent underscores the adult's awareness that he or she is now the responsible one. There will soon be no one else to refer decisions to. "The buck stops here."

Reaction to Panic: "Do Something!"

The reaction to this sense of loss and increased responsibility is quite likely to be panic, and an urge to "do something," anything, to change the situation.

Mr. Vargas, a storekeeper, accosted one of his regular customers with an urgent question: "Mrs. Phillips, you're a social worker. Tell me how I can prove my mother's citizenship. I can't find any papers and she's got to go into a nursing home." Mrs. Phillips, whose mind was on her family's dinner, was somewhat taken aback, but suggested that he call a friend of hers, who worked for an agency serving the elderly. When he did so, the story behind his request emerged: his mother, a peppery seventy-two-year-old, had fallen and sprained her ankle. Since then, she had been calling Mr. Vargas and his brother daily with complaints not only about her pain but about her landlord, her doctor, her neighbors, and the impossibility of getting a decent meal in such an environment. Her sons, alarmed by the onslaught, had inquired about nursing-home care and had been told that if she needed a subsidy, she must produce proof of citizenship. It turned out that she would not actually need to provide proof of citizenship—a "good-faith effort" to locate the documents would be sufficient.

When the agency worker visited Mrs. Vargas, however, the old lady made it plain that she had no intention of going to a nursing home or anywhere else. She was still limping and unable to manage stairs, but had an adequate supply of food brought by her sons in their weekly visits. She was angry about her discomfort and confinement to the house, and wanted to tell the world about it. In their

distress over her complaints, her sons had rushed to "do
something" that was not at all necessary. In their haste to
respond to what they perceived as her request, they had
acted very much as they used to as boys of ten or twelve,
when Mother was angry. Although they had learned, as
adults, to handle her peremptory demands with some degree of comfort, the stress of illness and potential disability
had revived the childhood wish to "please Mother," as well
as the fear of what would happen if they didn't. Consulting
an outside expert helped to reassure the sons that Mother
was not, in fact, in any serious jeopardy, and this reassurance
enabled them to restore the balance that had been threatened by her injury and consequent panic. Having an outsider listen to her story also reassured Mother that she was
not alone, that help was available if needed. In a calmer
mood, she concluded that she was not ready to make any
changes in her life style.

Ignorance Increases Panic

Mr. Vargas and his brother were successful businessmen,
used to judging the realities of the market and making decisions based on evidence. Yet in considering their mother's
needs they behaved like amateurs. This was partly because
they did not, in fact, know much about the resources available. In this, they were like most Americans. Many adults
who feel capable of choosing a house, a school, or a summer
camp draw a complete blank when faced with making a
decision about the need for a nursing home, let alone select-
ing one. It is a task for which they have no preparation,
and no information except the scare headlines in newspapers. This is another example of the cultural "invisibility"
of the elderly and their needs, which makes life difficult

not only for them but for their families as well.

Fortunately, this situation is changing. Many sources of information and help have recently come into being. Every state and many localities now have area agencies on aging, created by 1973 amendments to the Older Americans Act of 1965. These can provide much information on available services and resources and facilities for the elderly. (See Appendix IV.)

Denial: Another Reaction to Change

Some children, rather than seeing disaster in minor set-backs, go to the opposite extreme and refuse to acknowl-edge any change at all. The parent may be severely deterio-rated, malnourished, or incontinent, yet the child insists, "He was always like that; he never had much appetite," or, "It's up to her to decide what she wants to do." Such families are likely to be castigated as indifferent, but the truth may be that they are not uncaring but terrified. They, too, may benefit from professional help. To see the deterio-ration of someone we love and depend on is a heavy burden to carry alone. As sources of help proliferate, there is no need to carry the burden alone.

Becoming Caretakers

Not only is parental decline frightening because it implies increased responsibility and eventual loss—and is a re-minder to the younger adults of their own aging—but it also presents a puzzle. How does one provide care for those who have always been the care-givers? When the decision makers need help, how does one shift gears? Whatever the parents may have been—challenging or protective, strict or permissive—they were the reality against which their growing children tested themselves and braced themselves in order to develop their own individuality. Now, even when the child is fully grown, a change in the parents can leave the child feeling hollow, unsupported, almost weightless.

The film *I Never Sang for My Father* describes the efforts of two grown children to deal with their father after their mother's death. The old man is just as autocratic as ever, but not as capable. The son and daughter feel, uneasily, that "something ought to be done," but are reluctant to get more closely involved in a relationship that was always ungratifying for them, and are fearful of sacrificing the rest of their lives in a vain attempt to "please Dad." The son, in particular, feels his hard-won independence is threatened by his father's weakness. He had learned, painfully and over a long period of time, to establish his own priorities, which were quite different from his father's expectations, but always, in the background, was that strong and unrelenting presence. Now that his father is no longer strong, what is he to do? Must he allow himself to be thrust back into childhood by his father's wishes? Should he insist on measures which father wants no part of? Can he simply go on about his business and leave the old man to his own devices? Or what? If it is difficult to learn how to be a parent to one's children, it can be even harder to figure out how to be a child to one's aging parents and still maintain both one's own adulthood and theirs.

"Doing to Them as They Did to Us": The Ghosts in the Closet

When children become parents, they generally provide the same kind of care they were given. And if the parents in their turn need care, the grown children are also likely to follow the examples they were given. Thus a woman who, as a child, was constantly admonished to "eat your spinach, finish your oatmeal, clean your plate" may be very concerned, as an adult, about her mother's diet. "She eats like a bird, she doesn't get enough protein, she won't eat salad." One such determined daughter took Mother to her own home to make sure that she ate "properly," and lectured her daily about the importance of a balanced diet, until the old lady put a stop to it by moving back to her own apartment. The entire family then combined to convince Mother that she should have meals brought in. But Mother, whose speech was somewhat impaired, was nevertheless able to say no quite clearly. She finally compromised by accepting some part-time help with meal preparation on condition that the helper would stay and eat lunch with her. In their focus on food as the guarantee of good health, Mother and her family were playing out the roles of anxious parent and rebellious child, only in reverse. In similar fashion, some adult children are very concerned about their elders' bowel habits, and may seem to take a positive delight in giving enemas. They are likely to be the same children who were subjected to strenuous toilet training in their youth.

It is not only in such obvious matters as food and elimination and wearing galoshes that the old tapes get replayed. The more subtle attitudes of confidence or doubt, gratification or disappointment, which pervade the parent-child relationship in the growing years also operate later. Fathers and mothers who cheerfully expected their youngsters to achieve maturity, and who enjoyed them in the process, will probably get a calm and helpful reaction to their own situation, should they need help in later years.

Marcia Freeson, whom we met in Chapter I, is a good

example. Some years after the death of her husband, Will, she developed a thyroid malignancy. It was treated successfully, but the side effects of the treatment left her in a wheelchair. This was a severe blow to a woman as active as Marcia, but she did not give way to panic or bitterness. Her children, former foster children, and grandchildren, most of whom lived nearby, helped her to organize her life so that she could manage with minimal outside assistance. In this they probably took their cue from her lifelong attitude that "things will work out." When the children were of school age, the family was faced with the financial and emotional crisis of Will's sudden blindness. This meant a complete change of life style: a shift in career from chemistry to farming and a move from the city to an unimproved acreage near a small town. Will and Marcia were sure that, as a family, they could work it out together: they would make a living, the children would complete their education, and they would even have fun doing it. And they did. So when Marcia was struck by illness and disability, the family had had lots of practice in dealing with apparent disaster in creative ways.

The Impossible Dream

Many families are not so capable as the Freesons. They are dogged by the expectation, probably handed down to the third and fourth generation, that the worst is bound to happen and that they will be found wanting. Some children try, all their lives, to overcome the parental message that they are not quite good enough.

Viola Granger spent most of her life in competition with a ghost. When she was twenty-one, her sister Lily died suddenly of appendicitis. Their parents never got over it. For years, Viola heard about Lily's beauty, goodness, intelligence, and the terrible tragedy of her loss. She began to feel as if she had been somehow responsible for the death and that she was bound to make up for it to her parents. But no matter what she did, it was unfavorably compared with Lily's accomplishments, real or imagined. Lily made better grades; Lily would have had a more important career, married a smarter man, been a better mother. Viola became so convinced of her own inferiority that she did not, in fact, accomplish as much as she probably could have. When her mother broke a hip and her father was trying to care for her at home, Viola went every day to help out. But her efforts were not welcomed. "Don't worry so much," her father said. "You make me nervous." And her mother continued the old refrain: "*Lily* would have understood." Viola became more and more frantic in her efforts to prove that she was indeed a good daughter, more hopeless in her convictions that she never could succeed, and more fearful that if anything happened to her parents, she would be responsible. Finally, she called a family-counseling agency. "I don't know what to do," she told the social worker. "I'm afraid the only way out is to kill my parents and myself." The agency responded to her plea, and at long last she began to get help in recognizing, and eventually abandoning, the impossible dream—the perfect child, the perfect parents. It took a lot of work, for the habits of a lifetime are not easily changed. It is especially hard to give up the hope of parental approval.

The Hostile Elements of Overprotectiveness

Viola is an extreme example, but she illustrates several aspects of the bind that families get into when parents project their disappointments onto their children, and children try to live up to the implied parental expectations. In attempting to achieve the impossible dream, families ignore the available realities. Also, a continual effort to please someone else at one's own expense generates a lot of anger. It feels dangerous to acknowledge anger against someone who is loved and needed—it seems safer to turn the hostility against oneself, so that the anger becomes a chronic sense of guilt and self-blame. Another defense is to become very protective of the loved-and-hated person. Viola, who had plenty of cause to be angry about the parental messages that had so restricted her life, developed a morbid fear that "something would happen" to her parents, and worried constantly about every aspect of their lives. She was afraid that the visiting nurses who came to the home were neglecting or mistreating her mother, that the doctor's diagnosis was wrong, that her father would be unable to cope with the landlord or the Medicare forms. Although some of these concerns were legitimate, her constant fussing drove both her parents and their helpers to distraction. This not only enabled Viola to reassure herself that she was taking good care of her parents, but also provided her with a subtle but effective means of retaliation.

Such behavior is not confined to the relations between adults and their elderly parents. It frequently occurs in any situation in which the relationship is lopsided: that is, where the investment of energy far outweighs the gratification. It is common in parents of retarded or otherwise "difficult" children, where much care is required and not much reward can be expected in terms of the child's achievement. Such parents have to come to terms with the fact that their children will never completely "grow up," will always need some degree of care and protection, will not enter Harvard or become doctors or produce grandchildren. In their frustration, these parents often become more protective than is necessary or desirable. Spouses caring for severely disabled husbands or wives often suffer from the same conflict, as we saw earlier. What causes so much pain is the unacceptability of their anger at the unrewarding person: how can one be angry with the sick and helpless? The fact remains that anger is a natural human response to frustration, and if it is not acknowledged, it will be acted out.

When Independence Is Difficult to Accept

It is paradoxical that although the decline and dependency of one's parents is frightening, their continued independence may also cause anxiety. This is most apt to be true when the parents have begun to show some signs of impairment but are not severely disabled.

When the romance of Libby Franklin and David Galt (see page 22) began, for instance, Libby's son became quite anxious when David took Libby to a restaurant for dinner. He knew that his mother sometimes forgot appointments and that David tended to doze after dinner. He imagined David asleep in the restaurant and Libby unable to find her way home. Perhaps his concern was not so different from that of a father whose adolescent daughter is late from a date. When we know that our loved ones must face real risks, it threatens our sense of control. The "butterflies in the stomach" that we experience when Junior marches off to kindergarten, when his fifteen-year-old sister leaves for her first date, or when his grandmother insists, despite her angina pains, on traveling to California alone are not so different. They arise from the fact that we cannot, in fact, make the world totally safe for anybody. Having to recognize our finiteness in this respect is very frustrating, and undercuts our American assumption that everything can and should be made to turn out all right. If it doesn't, it means that somebody has failed, probably one of us.[3]

The Parallel Crisis of Adolescent Departure and Adult Decline

It is one of the hazards of middle life that the decline of one's parents often coincides with the emancipation of one's children. For better or worse, the children are leaving, or getting ready to leave, for college, jobs, marriage—in general, adulthood.

This may be a time of gratification and new freedom for their parents, but it is also a loss, and a reminder that their time of greatest influence is past. If, at the same time, the children's grandparents are experiencing ill health, widowhood, or some other stress, the combination can be a "double whammy" to the middle generation.

Mrs. Rosenquist experienced such a double whammy when, in the midst of the preparations for her daughter's wedding, her father died suddenly. His widow, whose memory had been failing noticeably for several years, began making heavy demands on her daughter's time and energy. It was not that the older woman was unable to manage her daily affairs—she did that quite well—but she was constantly calling for advice, reassurance, and company. Mrs. Rosenquist felt herself pulled in a dozen directions. She had no time to mourn for her father; the wedding was imminent; and her mother could not seem to make the slightest decision without her presence. She finally persuaded Mother to enter a nursing home, not because she needed

one medically but because it was the only way Mrs. Rosenquist could see to give herself breathing space. She felt
inadequate and guilty about not having been able to manage
all the crises at once, and sought solace by trying to convince
herself and others that her mother really did need nursing-
home care.

Often the conflicting demands are real and difficult to
juggle. However, sometimes the anxiety of adult sons and
daughters appears to spring from some source other than
the need of their elders.

Mr. and Mrs. Elston approached a home for the aged
to place an application for Mrs. Elston's mother, a seventy-
five-year-old woman living in her own apartment. Asked
why they felt she needed such a setting, the Elstons were
rather vague and general in their answers. They mentioned
arthritis and the fact that winter was coming. With slippery
streets, something might happen to the old lady. She really
shouldn't be alone at her age. Pressed to be more specific
as to why they were particularly concerned now, Mr. Elston
finally said, "My wife needs a rest. Every day she's over
at her mother's—if it isn't one thing it's another. She's been
like this ever since Buddy went away to college." From
further discussion, it appeared that Mrs. Elston's mother
was in her usual state of health and was not making any
additional requests, but that Mrs. Elston herself was feeling
at loose ends since the departure of the last child. To fill
the void, she had turned her attention to her mother, and
Mr. Elston was getting tired of it. Why couldn't she stay
home and pay attention to him? The empty-nest crisis was
thus converted into a concern about Grandma, and the
whole issue of the wife's new role and the relationship of
the couple was neatly side-stepped.

Sibling Rivalry Revisited

"Fussing over Grandma" can become a very complex activity when several children or grandchildren are involved. Not only are the needs of the elderly parent apt to be seen differently by each child, but the lifelong relationship among the children affects the way they react to those needs.

When Maria Hennessey began to show signs of failing health, her son Robert and her two married daughters, Mary Beth and Nan, found themselves embroiled in a dispute over what should be done about it. Although they began by considering Mrs. Hennessey's health and finances, the argument soon shifted to Robert's ability to keep a job and his motivation for living with Mother, Mary Beth's husband's ability to contribute, and the demands of Nan's children. Feeling themselves at a stalemate, they appealed to the oldest sister, Cecilia, a single professional woman living in another state, to come and straighten things out. She tried, but soon became the target of all the others. "You don't understand," they accused her. "Why are you being so bossy when you don't know anything about it?"

Finally, Nan, whose contributions had been less vitriolic, suggested calling in Dr. Matthew Whittaker, their family physician for many years. He had retired from active practice, but still lived in the neighborhood. He had always been a friend as well as a doctor, and the little Hennesseys had considered "Dr. Wick's" peppermint drops a sure cure for bruised feelings as well as for skinned knees and sneezes.

He came and listened. When he had heard everybody's story, he turned to Maria Hennessey, who had been silent.

"Well, Maria, what do you think we should do?" Mrs. Hennessey twisted her fingers in her lap for a long moment. "I don't know, Matt," she answered finally. "I feel all right—we're managing." Her voice regained a trace of its old tartness: "I really don't know what they're making such a fuss about."

Dr. Whittaker looked at the assembled group of grown-up children. "Well, my dears," he said, as he had so often said to their mother when faced with a questionable rash or stomach ache, "let's be brave and do nothing." Laughter at the familiar saying helped to reduce the intensity of the confrontation between the brother and sisters, and to restore some perspective about the original cause of their concern.

"Dr. Wick" was able to reassure the children that Mrs. Hennessey was basically in good health, despite the increasing discomfort of her arthritis. He offered to keep an eye on her and to let them know if any more disturbing symptoms appeared. Since Mrs. Hennessey insisted that she was managing well financially and needed no help from the children, the doctor also encouraged them in the idea of setting up a contingency trust fund, to which they would all contribute but which would be administered by the bank rather than by any of the siblings. Thus assured that the situation was not so critical, as well as that they had a means for "doing something," the family were able to relinquish their quarrel.

The Hennesseys are an example of how difficult it can be for people to step out of the roles they have assumed or been assigned as siblings and parents. They also illustrate the pitfalls of appointing one sibling to be the speaker or the organizer when there is family conflict. An outsider who has or can gain the confidence of the whole group is in a better position to help them separate the old feelings from the current issues.

"It Has to Be Done, but I Don't Want to Be the One to Do It"

Another kind of sibling conflict arises when the family sees no alternative to institutional care, but no one wants to be responsible for initiating it. Mother or Father may be shunted back and forth among several children, none of them really able to provide adequate care, while they blame each other for the deterioration that they see. Or one may decide to arrange for nursing-home care and another rush in with the declaration "You'll never do that to my mother," then rush off again without having contributed any further to making a plan. Sometimes children visit a parent who is living in the home of another child, only to commiserate with him or her over the "meanness" of the caretaker! The same thing often happens if the parent is institutionalized, but then it is likely to be the institution that gets the blame.

Children who are actively involved in caretaking and who are subject to a barrage of criticism from the non-caretakers are naturally resentful. Whether they fight back or withdraw from communication with the critics, their burdens are heavier than need be. What families who spend a lot of time and energy sniping at each other usually fail to realize is that all of them, the involved and the uninvolved alike, are struggling with a heavy burden of guilt. They deal with it in the only way they know how, by trying to shove it on someone else. Often an outsider can help them deal with and resolve the guilt, rather than pass it around like a hot potato. This, in turn, can free them to cope more effectively with the real situation.

Why Do We Feel Guilty?

Part of the middle generation's discomfort arises from the feeling that they have failed to meet their parents' expectations. It is, in fact, becoming less common for extended families to live in the same household, or even the same part of the country. Parents may be disappointed that they do not get the kind of attention that elders got when they were young. However, that is only part of the story. Children may, indeed, agonize over taking a job or moving to another part of the country, but under the reality lurks the feeling that they should be able to keep their parents from deteriorating. They assume, without really acknowledging the feeling, that if they were really "good children," Mother wouldn't have arthritis, Father wouldn't be bored with his retirement, and everybody would be happy. This, of course, is nonsense. Nobody can stop time, and nobody can create happiness for another person—neither parent, child, nor spouse. But the sense of obligation to do so underlies much middle-aged anxiety about aging parents. Such an unrealistic sense of responsibility is particularly burdensome for those whose parents always lived vicariously, who expected their fulfillment to come from their spouses' success or their children's accomplishments. If they never learned to create their own happiness, neither their children nor anyone elso can do it for them. Their dissatisfaction and disappointment are painful to watch, but their children's burdens may be somewhat eased by the realization that for this, at least, they are not responsible.

Faced with the apparently conflicting needs and expecta-

tions of the different generations, children and parents
sometimes try to conceal them from each other in an effort
to escape the conflict. This seldom works very well. The
feelings are still there, and get themselves expressed in one
way or another.

Mother may have strong opinions about her daughter's
job, her son-in-law's smoking, and her grandchildren's up-
bringing, while she prides herself on her noninterference:
"I never say anything." Yet she calls constantly with "inno-
cent" inquiries—"Did you know there's a tornado watch
this afternoon? I suppose the children are home alone. Did
you see the *Reader's Digest* article on how to help your
husband to stop smoking? Did the children go to Sunday
School this week?" Such inquiries often make the family
fume. "I know she means well," her daughter may say,
"but sometimes she makes me feel about six years old, with
dirty fingernails." Nevertheless, she and the rest of the family feel guilty about pushing Mother away. So they answer
the questions patiently, being careful not to express irrita-
tion. They keep visits short, pleading a busy schedule. As
a result of this non-dialogue, Mother feels rejected and
members of the family feel put upon. Having carefully con-
cealed their real feelings, each wonders why the others
are not aware of them, and the elaborate shadowboxing
match continues.

Rather than resorting to subterfuge, a frank recognition
of the differences can often ease the hidden resentment.
In spite of the difficulties, children and parents *can* learn
to talk to each other, and even enjoy each other. One generation's solution need not become the other's problem.

6

How to Enjoy the Generation Gap

Each stage in our journey through life brings both losses and gains, not just to ourselves but to our families as well. A young girl who goes off to college, for instance, gives up the security of home but gains a new sense of independence and freedom. Her family will feel the separation keenly, but will also experience a sense of relief from obligation and worry. Thus Mother, who slept fitfully until Donna was safely home after the high-school basketball game, sleeps soundly now, despite her awareness of Donna's late campus hours and her own empty nest.

Not only as the young grow up but also as the mature grow old do changes in one generation have repercussions for all the others in the family. This is most pronounced at such points of change as retirement or the decision of a retiree to return to work, widowhood or remarriage, illness or recovery. But even when there are no dramatic events and the shifts from one phase of life to another are not characterized by obvious landmarks, the concerns and attitudes that surface often resemble being on a seesaw. A young person can feel and act childish in some ways and grown-up in others; by the same token, the shift from middle to old age has the same qualities, as the adults begin to see themselves as old in some ways while remaining and thinking young in others. In neither generation is it possible to predict the inconsistencies exactly, although it is consistent with the way life progresses that they will occur. And while there are no sharp lines of demarcation between youth and maturity or maturity and old age, there are parallel concerns which all generations share. Discovering these similarities may facilitate the communication between the generations, bridge the gaps, and help in the resolution of shared conflicts. Some of the most common of these concerns, listed below, could well serve as a reminder of John Donne's words, that "No man is an island."

PARALLEL CONCERNS

Middle Generation (40–70)	*Older Generation* (60–90+)
1. How can I get my children/parents to listen to me?	1. Who listens to old people?
2. How can I balance all my responsibilities?	2. Who will take care of me?
3. How can I have a life of my own?	3. How can I stay independent?
4. How can I do something meaningful with my life while there is still time?	4. How can I continue to be myself despite all these changes?
5. How can I stop feeling so guilty?	5. What has my life been worth?
6. How can I shed the dread of knowing that Mother/Father might die soon?	6. We all have to go sometime, but will I be ready when my time comes?

Even when we sense that our parents' or children's concerns are similar to ours, it is not always easy to share our feelings. Old habits as well as old grievances get in the way. Communication is a skill that must be learned, and learning takes practice.

Communications: Learning to Listen

Everybody complains that nobody listens. Parents complain about their children and children about their parents. Husbands and wives complain about each other. Everybody wants an audience, but nobody wants to be one. Why?

All too often, the limits of our patience to listen are severely tested. "I've heard it a million times" is a common refrain or a frequently unspoken thought. Grandpa's arthritis, father's politics, mother's complaints about meat prices, daughter's enthusiasm over a dress or a football player—all these may seem too familiar and commonplace to be worth attention. They become a kind of background music to our own preoccupations. There is no new information to be gained.

Talk, however, is a means of providing information as well as seeking recognition. If others do not respond to what we have to say, we feel put down and are likely to be less interested in what they have to say.

Mr. Lawrence came into the kitchen when his daughter Nancy was getting supper. "Brought you the paper," he said. "I see there's been another of those arson fires."

"Dad, I haven't got time to look at a paper now." Nancy did not turn from the stove. "And I do wish you would wipe your feet when you come in."

Mr. Lawrence left the kitchen without another word, and without wiping his feet.

While such methods of noncommunication can be bluntly stated, as Nancy did, or unspoken but expressed through action or nonaction, as was Mr. Lawrence's way, fortunately the system also works in reverse. Shutting out invites retaliation, but recognition promotes response.

Tom Blake sometimes thought he would strangle his mother if he had to sit through another account of her shopping trips. Every store, every salesgirl, every discovery of shoddy merchandise or triumphant discovery of a bargain was described in detail. And she went shopping every day! Tom, who never went into a store if he could avoid it, usually fidgeted through these recitals, taking refuge in the sports page if his son hadn't grabbed it before he got home, and saying "Um" once in a while.

One day he tried something different. He put the paper down and looked at his mother while she talked. When she finished her story, he commented, "You must have had an interesting day." His mother looked startled. "I didn't know you were interested in shopping," she said. Tom felt a moment of panic, but decided to stick with the truth. "I'm not, really," he ventured, "but I'm glad you had a good time."

Mother smiled and gathered up her packages. "Well," she said, "it filled up the time. Now I'd better put these things away." Then, noting his glance at the headlines, "Go on and read your paper. You must be tired."

Those who are subjected to repetitious stories, as Tom was, may fear that any encouragement will open the floodgates and that they would never get anything done—much less get in a word themselves. However, the reverse is true. After a period—even a short period—of *real* attention, one can say, "Now I have to go," or, "Now I want to tell you something." It is the quality, not the quantity, of listening that matters. One can and must define what the limits are, for nobody can do everything that everybody else wants. Saying "No more now" after a time of listening and responding is much easier for the other person to accept than is the silent "No" of constant inattention.

Listening can be especially hard when the speaker's whole repertoire seems to consist of complaints and grievances. But even in such cases, understanding the reasons and the need, and drawing the line when "one has had enough" can make life easier for the listener and, in time, even the complainer.

Naomi Kahler's aches and pains could take all day to describe, and often did. Her daughter dreaded her phone calls—interminable, repetitious, and guilt-provoking. For a long time she tried to tune them out by thinking about something else, but she still felt miserable afterward. She tried arguing that the pain wasn't really so bad, but that only produced tears, recriminations, and more symptoms. Finally she learned to acknowledge what her mother was saying and to respond to it, but also to limit the time on the phone. "It sounds like you really feel bad—I'm sorry. Can I get you anything?" After a few minutes she could say, "I can't talk any more now, Mother. I'll call you tomorrow." She also discovered that if she initiated the calls, they were shorter and less traumatic. She could select the time that was easier for her and spend ten or fifteen minutes, rather than being bombarded for an hour with saved-up grievances and Mother's full agenda.

If we want to be listened to, we have to do some listening. But what about the message we want to send? How can it be conveyed most effectively?

Communications: Sending Clear Messages

Sometimes the signals get lost because people do not convey their needs and wishes directly. This makes it difficult for the listeners to respond. Grandpa may assume, "They should know what I want if they love me," and then be hurt and angry if he doesn't get it. His loved ones, not having a crystal ball, are confused and put off by the anger. "Grandpa is so unreasonable," they may say. "He must be getting senile." Meanwhile, Grandpa fumes that "young people are so inconsiderate." Neither youth nor age is the culprit, however. At any age, we have to say what we want if others are to know what it is.

Melissa Wyman, after she retired, was dismayed by the rapidity with which inflation was eating up her Social Security check. She had some savings, but was very fearful about how long she would be able to manage, especially if she got sick. She hesitated to talk to her children about the problem. What if they couldn't help, or were not even interested? She shared her worries with a group of friends, who encouraged her to try anyhow. With considerable trepidation, she told her two daughters and her son about the problem. They all responded warmly. Of course they would help if she needed them. They considered setting up a contingency fund, but Melissa felt that was not necessary— she just wanted to know that help was available. The children decided to go ahead anyway and set up a savings account for Mother to which they would all contribute. They had not realized that she was worried, or that her financial cushion was so small, until she told them.

The reluctance to be direct may stem not only from the assumption that our wishes are known, but from the fear that our demands are too great. I don't want to be a burden, thinks Grandma; so instead of saying "I need help," she only hints. Then if the hint isn't taken, she feels neglected. Like Melissa Wyman, she may require active encouragement to express her needs and concerns.

Sometimes the problems, fears, or feelings are shared with

only one part of the family. Mr. and Mrs. Morrison, an old couple beset by many physical problems, turned to their son Kurt for help with shopping, food preparation, and other personal services. They had another son, Ron, but did not want to ask him for anything because he was deaf. Despite his handicap, however, he had a job, a wife and family, and had certainly proved himself to be a capable person.

Kurt and his wife, feeling overwhelmed by the amount of help they were being asked to provide, finally persuaded the Morrisons that Ron should be involved, too. When approached, Ron and his wife were not only willing to help, but hurt because the problem hadn't been shared with them sooner. "Is something wrong with us? Aren't we part of this family?" they asked plaintively. The Morrisons had been denying themselves help that was available, and overburdening one of their children quite unnecessarily. As a result of their protective stance, both sons felt resentful. When the problem was discussed openly, it turned out to be more manageable than anybody had thought. Not only did the old people get more help, but the relationships between all the family members improved. Visits and outings began to happen that had previously been avoided because of hidden resentment.

Both older and younger people sometimes avoid discussion of illness or other family problems so as not to "worry" each other. But the ones who are being kept in the dark usually sense that something is amiss, and worry even more because they don't know what it is. Sharing the problem, however bad it may be, removes the nightmare quality of isolation.

Rita Kleban had just received very bad news. Her cancer, which had been treated surgically several years earlier, had recurred and spread. Although some means of treatment were still available, her chances of survival were not very good. Rita was stunned, not only for herself but for her family—her husband, teenage son, and mother. How could she lay such news on them? And how could she bear it alone?

Fortunately for Rita and her family, she didn't try to deal with it alone. She and her husband talked and cried together, and felt closer in their shared distress. They debated whether to tell fourteen-year-old Jonathan, who resolved the question for them by appearing in the middle of one such discussion to ask, "What's wrong with Mom?" Although dismayed by the answer, he surprised them by voluntarily taking on household chores that he had previously ignored. When his father commended him, his response was "Well, you and Mom need me now." He also grew an incredible three inches in the course of his mother's chemotherapy treatments. Perhaps this was a physical expression of the effects of being treated like an adult and a participating member of the family. We have been told for years that diseases such as heart attacks, ulcers, and arthritis can be caused by unresolved emotional stress. Is it not possible that emotional growth also has physical consequences?

In much the same way, Rita's mother drew closer to the family circle when Rita finally brought herself to tell her about the illness. Mother gladly agreed to go along when Rita asked her to accompany her to the treatments, and far from feeling, as Rita had feared, that her daughter and fate had let her down, she was gratified that her child once more needed her. Resuming the maternal role gave her a means of coping with her grief over the illness. Like her grandson, she discovered the joy of standing taller as they dealt with the family tragedy together.

It is a paradox that lesser crises than the one the Klebans faced may be harder to share. A financial setback, a physical ailment that is more embarrassing than disabling, a personal disappointment—such things may seem "unnecessary" to discuss with parents, spouses, or children. A sense of guilt may interfere with such sharing. We sometimes feel that the difficult situation should not have happened, or that we should be able to deal with it alone, or that others should not be expected to respond to troubles which they had no share in creating. Yet, as the Morrisons and the Klebans both illustrate, open discussion not only facilitates a solution but also promotes a more enjoyable relationship. It can work just as well with smaller problems, as well as provide practice for dealing with larger ones. A successful family is not one to which nothing bad ever happens; it is one in which, no matter what happens, the members remain available to each other and share in coping with it.

Headaches Versus Heartaches

Physical aches and pains are often considered more legitimate than emotional ones. Naomi Kahler (see page 139), for instance, had a hard time saying that she was lonely, or that she was frightened by her increasing immobility. So she described the arthritis in exhaustive detail, then was offended if the listener suggested she see her doctor. If the doctor prescribed aspirin and hot baths, she felt even more put upon. What she really wanted was a friendly voice, a comforting presence—someone to rub her back and reassure her that she was not alone. But because she did not know how to say so, her neighbors and her daughter found it confusing and frustrating to try to help her.

Another old lady told a group of her friends that her children were very attentive when she was sick—not so attentive when she was lonely. They agreed that their experience was similar. Since we are accustomed to paying more attention to physical than to emotional needs, perhaps the "loneliness" message has to be made particularly loud and clear. How can this be done?

It is often easier to share one's concerns with family after discussing them with peers. Those who work with adolescents are well aware of this, and there is no reason why elderly and middle-aged folk should not avail themselves of the same resource. Some such groups are already in existence. It is not necessary, however, to wait for a formal group to be established. Neighbors and friends may be able to provide support and clarification for what one would like to say to Mother or Dad or son or daughter.

Another family member may recognize what is happening and help to put it into words. Grandmother's fears and loneliness may be more obvious to a grandchild, a nephew, or someone else less intimately involved with Grandmother or her children. Such a person may be able to act as a "bridge" or facilitator of communication. Or perhaps a non-family professional, such as a social worker, clergyman, or doctor, may be best equipped to help sort out the issues and identify the cry for companionship hidden under the physical complaints.

To See Ourselves as Others See Us

One of the advantages of talking to each other is getting feedback about ourselves. We are likely to be in for some surprises. What we have supposed was an effort to protect

others from our feelings may be perceived by them as cold-
ness or unwillingness to share. On the other hand, qualities
we were not even aware of may be appreciated and enjoyed
by those around us.

Helen Hendricks, a widow in her sixties, took time out
from attending a conference on aging to have dinner with
her grandson and his wife. Encouraged by what she had
heard at the meetings, she asked them, "Well, what do
you think of me as an aging grandmother?" The young
people looked surprised. Then her grandson responded,
"Gee . . . we think you're neat!" They went on to tell her
of their admiration for her intelligence and energy, and,
above all, how much they enjoyed her funny stories. They
probably would not have thought to tell her if she hadn't
asked.

Sometimes, of course, the feedback is not so pleasant.
We may be driving our relatives up the wall, and vice versa.
Even so, there is more chance to correct the situation if
we know it exists.

Katie Green had always been a managing sort of person,
who knew what was best for everybody, especially her children. As aging increased her physical frailty, she fought back
by telling her daughter how to run her life, and by constant
complaining about her physical miseries. "Somebody should
do something" was the message her family received.

Her daughter Marcy decided that perhaps Mama needed
nursing-home care, and applied to an agency for help in
finding an appropriate facility. The young man who visited
to discuss the situation, however, pointed out that Mrs.
Green was actually caring for herself very well. "But she's
always telling me how poorly she feels, and that I don't
help her enough," said Marcy, puzzled.

Mrs. Green turned to the visitor. "She stays half an hour and runs away," she commented disapprovingly. "Always watching the clock."

"Well," said the visitor, with a smile, "if all I heard was complaints and criticisms, I wouldn't want to stay either."

Marcy was rather shocked by such forthrightness, but Katie Green laughed heartily. "I like you, young feller," she said. "Most young folks are too mealy-mouthed."

Further discussion helped Mrs. Green to develop other topics of conversation besides her own miseries, and this led to more gratifying relationships with her family and neighbors. The process required a number of interviews, as well as considerable willingness on Mrs. Green's part to practice the new skills. Changes in personal style do not happen overnight. But they can happen.

As in Mrs. Green's case, it may be easier for an outsider to point out the behavior that is making relationships difficult than for those embroiled in the dispute to do so. But family members themselves can identify what bothers them and how they would like to see it changed. It helps to put the request in positive rather than negative terms: "I wish you'd call later in the evening instead of suppertime" rather than "I wish you'd leave me alone!"

The Overloaded Fuse: Dealing with Demands

Sometimes it seems as if everybody wants everything. Children, parents, spouses, friends, employers, organizations, causes—everywhere we turn there are needs crying to be met. It is easy to assume that we have to jump in and meet all of them, but this is a fallacy. Nobody can attempt to fulfill all the requests that come his way without denying his own needs for privacy, replenishment, personal space—a life of his own. In protest against so much encroachment on our own personalities, we may ignore the requests, agree to "do something" but fail to follow through, or respond with increasing irritability and resentment. There are better ways.

Acknowledgment Versus Action

Not all wishes can be fulfilled. The person confined to bed or wheelchair longs to walk again; the blind person yearns for the restoration of his vision. Neither may be possible; yet the wish is both real and natural. It is kinder to acknowledge the wish while admitting its impossibility than to deny it altogether. "Yes, I know—I wish so, too" is more supportive than "Well, you can't, so there's no use wishing." Then one can assist in the search for substitute gratifications while admitting that they *are* substitutes.

When Will Freeson (see page 14) lost his sight, his wife, Marcia, made a habit of describing the scene to him wherever they happened to be, thus helping him to maintain a visual sense of where he was. Children, neighbors, and other associates followed Marcia's lead, in a matter-of-fact way, without self-consciousness or expressions of pity. As a result, Will and all those who knew him felt less helpless about dealing with the situation.

Sometimes the wish is for more of someone's time and energy than can be made available. Again it is more supportive to acknowledge the wish than to argue with it. This does not mean that the wish can be fulfilled, however.

Mary Barton, age seventy-nine, had a particularly severe case of spinal arthritis. Her back was so twisted that she had a difficult time walking, even in her own apartment. Her niece Julie helped by picking up groceries for her and getting the laundry done. Aunt Mary managed her household tasks herself, although slowly, and all went well until Julie told her that she planned to be away for a three-week vacation trip. Aunt Mary was indignant. "How can you do this to me, a sick old woman?" she stormed. In vain, Julie explained that the laundry could be sent out, and that she could arrange with a nearby store to have groceries delivered. She offered to have her friend Karen, who worked in Julie's office, call during her absence to make sure that all was well. Aunt Mary protested that the store might send the wrong things, the laundry would ruin her clothes, and that the friend ("that young whippersnapper") probably wouldn't even remember to call.

Julie was distressed. Should she cancel her plans? After a sleepless night, she decided that she could not do that. She needed the vacation. "I know you'll miss me," she told her aunt. "I'm sorry I can't be in two places at once. Maybe the help you get won't be quite what you're used to, but I want you to have what you need. Suppose I bring Karen to meet you before I leave?"

Aunt Mary continued to mutter, but she accepted the situation, and was even gracious to Karen. Nothing unpleasant happened during Julie's absence, and when she returned, Aunt Mary twitted her about Karen's thoughtfulness—"better than some people I know." It was, perhaps, her way of admitting that two helpers could be better than one.

When Aunt Mary's wish that Julie should not leave was acknowledged, she was able to accept the proposed substitute, although grudgingly. Sometimes the substitute is not accepted. Another Aunt Mary might have preferred to do without or even to make her own arrangements. When we have been the mainstay for those who have to be dependent, it is easy to underestimate the resourcefulness of which they may still be capable.

When Action Is Requested, Then Refused

A complaint which sounds like a demand for action may in fact be a plea for acknowledgment of feeling. Mrs. Mecklenberg (see page 1), for instance, had complained so much about the discomforts of her life in Michigan City that her daughter assumed she was asking for a more protected environment—either her daughter's home or an institution of some kind. Mrs. Mecklenberg herself had denied that that was the case—"I tell her the news and she thinks the world is coming to an end," she had said. Nevertheless, daughter explored several alternative living arrangements. When, for each of them, Mrs. Mecklenberg first expressed interest, then backed off, daughter concluded: "She wants to make sure I'll be available when the time comes. But she'll let me know when that is."

The off-again on-again response is often very frustrating, both to old people who are expressing discomfort and to the relatives who are trying to help. "My brother spent so much time making arrangements for me to enter that retirement home," an old gentleman confided to one of his cronies. "If I tell him I don't want to go, he'll be furious." Brother may or may not be furious, but he is almost certain to be confused. "What *does* he want, for goodness' sake?" he may ask plaintively. And then, perhaps, "He really must be getting senile."

Indecision in the elderly is often ascribed to "senility" or "the aging process." We forget how many younger folks have second thoughts about buying a house, taking a job, or sticking with a marriage. Considering a change in life style in the later years creates as many mixed feelings as did the major decisions of the earlier years.

It helps to recognize and to talk about the disadvantages as well as the advantages of any proposed plan. For instance, moving to a retirement hotel may mean giving up the tasks of cooking, cleaning, and shopping. Is this seen as a loss or a gain? The new friends and social activities made possible by the new setting require an investment in getting acquainted with strangers, risking rejection or disappointment, and leaving the comfort of a familiar environment. The qualms experienced by a child entering a new school are just as real for the old person contemplating change. Both can be helped by recognition that there are negatives as well as positives, and that it is natural to feel scared and uncertain in a new situation. Trying to make the discomfort go away by stressing the positives only drives the feelings underground and makes the person experiencing them feel unacceptable and ungrateful. It is also likely to result in sabotage of the plan—a hasty cancellation, an "unreasonable" rejection of what seemed so reasonable and necessary. A frank discussion of the pros and cons also reduces the feeling of helplessness which is often the core of the discomfort. Being involved in the decision-making process gives one a sense of once more being in control of his life, rather than a helpless pawn of fate.

Setting Limits Versus Withdrawal

When the needs of others seem overwhelming, one way that people sometimes try to deal with the excessive demand is by withdrawing. Bombarded by requests for more and more service, those who have tried to help become frustrated, especially if the requests are accompanied by complaints and recriminations. Helpers get discouraged and angry. They stop visiting or are "too busy" to answer phone calls. They may move to another building—even another city—to escape the demands of an importunate neighbor or relative. Although such actions reduce the pressure, they are likely to leave the would-be helper feeling guilty and unsuccessful, as well as to decrease the supports of the person who needs help.

Limits can be set without resorting to such drastic measures. As Julie discovered with her Aunt Mary, it is quite possible to say, "No, I can't do everything." This is true whether the request comes from a parent, a child, or the president of the P.T.A.

Margaret McClendon (see page 53) was aware that no one person could do everything for her, and so she called upon many—her neighbors, friends, and church—to help her in dealing with the effects of a stroke. She knew she would only drive helpers away by leaning too heavily on them. Her solution was to diversify, to divide the necessary tasks among several people. Not all those in need are as wise as she, but they may be helped to extend their support network rather than overloading one or two people. Their helpers can assist in this process by setting realistic limits to what they can do. It may be comfortable to visit once a week, but not three times; to do the shopping, but not the laundry and the housecleaning; to talk on the phone for a few minutes, but not for an hour every day. What makes limit-setting difficult is the fact that we so often feel guilty about it.

How to Say No Without Feeling Guilty

Guilt is a necessary ingredient in the process of becoming a social being. Those who have none are without morals, unconcerned about the effects of their behavior on others.

They are as truly disabled as the victims of vitamin or hormone deficiencies—and much more dangerous. Too much guilt, however, is also a handicap. Its victims may be so preoccupied with their sense of obligation to others that they do not feel entitled to any needs of their own. They might profit by the comment of a small boy who was told by his Sunday School teacher that "we were put here on earth for the sake of others." After thinking that over, the youngster responded, "Then what are the others for?"

Guilt develops as children attempt, more or less successfully, to set aside their own wishes and please their parents. It may be reinforced in adulthood as parents attempt to meet the needs of their children. No one is completely successful in either effort, but most of us persist in feeling that we "should" be. The sense of guilt is most intense in those conflict-ridden relationships where the child has never felt successful in pleasing the parent. Resentment toward the parent who cannot be pleased is compounded by guilt over the resentment. The result may be ever more frantic efforts to "please"—often without reference either to one's own real needs or to the other person's.

A middle-aged daughter expressed a great deal of concern for her widowed father, visiting daily and trying to do many things that he preferred to do for himself. Asked why she felt constrained to perform all these services, she blurted out, "Because I can't stand him!" She was startled to discover how much of her solicitude stemmed from anger. She had always felt that her father considered her an incompetent bungler, and she was determined to prove that she could take good care of him. Whether he wanted or needed the care was beside the point.

Adult children are not the only ones who suffer unnecessary anguish in trying to make up for past deficits, real or imagined. The elderly parent may also feel a sense of guilty obligation to the child—particularly if the relationship has always been difficult or the child is disabled in some way. Fathers and mothers in their eighties and nineties struggle to continue caring for retarded sons and daughters who have always lived at home, and worry about what will happen when they are no longer there to do it. Eventually some crisis such as the illness of the caretaker may make other arrangements necessary. It is noteworthy that the retarded or otherwise disabled person frequently functions better outside the home environment, and may even begin to demonstrate unsuspected skills. The parents' lifelong efforts to provide care may have had more to do with their feelings of guilt about the disability than with the child's actual need for care.

It is sometimes said that when the relationship between children and parents is good, the issue of setting limits does not arise, and help is provided without resentment. To the extent that this is true, it is because in a good relationship both parties assume that each has legitimate needs. Limit-setting need not become an issue when the limits are built in. It is when one person feels that another is his "property," or that the obligation owed him is unlimited, that resentment and guilt become a problem.

Guilt often pushes us to do things for people that we don't want to do, and that they may not even need. How can we break the vicious cycle?

The first step is to take stock of our own needs—for rest, recuperation, privacy, creativity, other relationships, or whatever we feel is essential to our well-being. The second is to consider the needs of the other person—not what he wants or is accustomed to, necessarily, but what he needs. Julie's Aunt Mary, for instance, needed help in getting the groceries into the house and in getting her clothes washed. She also needed the reassurance of someone's concern and availability. She supposed that her only possible resource for these services was Julie, but that was not the case. In fact, the use of alternatives expanded her support network rather than restricting it.

The third step, therefore, is to consider how the identified needs can be met. The greatest obstacle to that process is the feeling that we "ought" to be able to provide everything, and that the other person is being deprived and restricted if we don't. It is ironic that feeling so terribly responsible can immobilize and prevent one from taking any constructive action. If Julie had believed that she, and she alone, was able to help Aunt Mary, she might have moved out of town rather than continue to bear such a global burden!

It is essential to remember that limiting one resource may expand another. As we know, when a child goes off to school, the time he spends with his mother is reduced, but his opportunities for new experience and learning are greatly increased. This means a loss and a gain for both mother and child—a change that can, and usually does, promote the development of both. In the same way, Aunt Mary and Julie both gained more freedom as a result of finding alternative sources of help.

Keeping in mind that change does not necessarily mean deprivation helps to reduce the burden of guilt. However, guilt is so prevalent in our society—and there are so many societal expecations that tend to reinforce it—that the individual, young or old, who is trying to cope with multiple responsibilities may need help in sorting out what the real issues are.

The Protectiveness Trap, and How to Get Out of It

It is difficult not to be seduced by those who appeal for help. The message they send can range from "I'm desperate—do something!" to "You are so good to me . . . you are the only one who understands . . . you light up my life." Child or parent, spouse or friend may be sending the message: "Because I am in need, you are responsible for meeting that need." If the message is accepted, the receiver takes on the immense burden of total responsibility for another's well-being. Feeling indispensable is very flattering, but also frightening. And well it may be, for no one actually has that much power. To assume that one does can only result in bitter disappointment on both sides. No one can be totally responsible for another's happiness, success, or health.

But suppose one is already in the position of trying to meet such expectations. Is there a way out?

The first step is to recognize and accept one's finiteness. This is often difficult, for the temptation to play God in another's life can be very powerful. It is, however, possible to change one's self-image, and this accomplishment can bring immense relief.

Margie Ross was sure that if the phone rang once more, her head would split. Either it would be the school, demanding to know why Dan, her fifteen-year-old son, was cutting class again, or it would be her mother with another shopping list. Ever since she had had a siege of flu early in the winter, her seventy-five-year-old mother had been depending on Margie for her grocery-shopping and other errands. She did not feel up to pulling a cart through the icy streets, so Margie had been going over on the weekends. It cut into her already crowded Saturdays, and she worried about being away from home for so many hours at a stretch. Dan and Christy, Margie's daughter, were certainly old enough to make their own sandwiches, but they always seemed to be tormenting each other.

Margie's thoughts returned uneasily to Dan's school problem. It would never do for Mother to know that Dan was cutting classes and ignoring his homework. Mother already worried too much about Margie's ability to manage the kids and a full-time job since the death of Margie's husband, Bill, five years earlier. Margie was also worried. There just isn't enough of me to go around, she thought wearily.

"Mom!" Twelve-year-old Christy appeared in the doorway. "Can I go swimming with Jean and Lori?"

"Did you finish cleaning your room?"

"No, but . . ."

"I told you yesterday that you'd have to get the junk off the floor before you went anywhere."

"Oh, Mom! They want to leave right away!"

"I told you. . . ."

Christy burst into tears. "You never make Dan do anything. What a crummy family!" She stormed out of the room and up the stairs.

Margie laid her head on her arms, feeling totally inadequate. And then the phone rang. She reached for it, bracing herself for the inevitable demand.

But it wasn't the school, or Dan, or Mother. It was Margie's best friend, Carla. Confronted with a sympathetic listener, Margie could not resist pouring out her tale of constant concern and discouragement. "No matter what I do, it isn't enough," she finished.

"Well, for goodness' sake!" Carla responded. "Do you think you have to do it all? You sound like one of those TV series where everything goes wrong in the first fifteen minutes and is supposed to turn out all right by the end of the hour."

Margie laughed ruefully. "Maybe you're right. . . . Maybe I don't have to write the whole script myself."

It would be untrue to imply that one telephone conversation changed Margie's whole outlook on life, or that she and her family lived happily ever after as a result. Such testimonials are the province of TV commercials and other faith healers. What is true, however, is that one's assumptions about oneself and the world can be modified by encounters with other people. The growth of personality is the result of such encounters as they occur throughout a lifetime, and even a lifetime is not long enough to fulfill the potential for growth we all have within us.

The Mirage of Perfection

Perfection is neither possible nor necessary to the growth process. Despite earnest efforts, there are bound to be disappointments and failures, anxiety and frustration. So what else is new? There is always room for improvement and the possibility of greater effectiveness, comfort, enjoyment, or whatever. To take perfect communication and/or perfect harmony as goals of family life is both unrealistic and self-defeating.

One expectation that burdens those who try to protect everybody is that everything should look "nice" and that nobody should be frustrated. The object of family or inter-generational communication, however, is not to present a smooth and harmonious success story, but to help everybody get his/her needs met. If that involves shouting, arguments, and anger, nobody is likely to die of it. What damages people is not anger but contempt—being demeaned or put down because of one's wishes or feelings. "I'm angry" is not demeaning, but "You're no good" is. It is one of the paradoxes of our culture that those who are burdened by feelings of responsibility for others often have the most difficulty in taking responsibility for their own feelings.

The Effective Use of Anger

When people are frustrated, they get angry, but because our society frowns on expressions of anger, the feeling is often disguised. One of the most common disguises is blaming somebody else for one's own feelings. A child who has been scolded may discharge his anger by calling his sister "stupid" or kicking the cat. Likewise, an executive who has lost a contract may fume at his secretary or his wife. Once started, the process can lead to an endless circle of recriminations and attempts to "get even." The result is to make everybody feel put down, and to look for someone else to punish so as to get out of the "down" position.

This kind of musical-chairs approach does not have much effect in changing the behavior that caused the anger in the first place. It is, in fact, more likely to reinforce it. A more effective method is to describe one's own feelings rather than the other person's motives or character. "It makes me mad when you don't call" is both clearer and less denigrating than "You don't care anything about me—you're thoughtless and ungrateful." Sharing one's feelings is also more likely to bring the desired response—an open reaction to an honest statement.

Old Dogs Can Learn New Tricks

Even when communication has been difficult for a long time, the parties involved can learn to change it. We tend to assume that only young people can change, while old people are rigid and inflexible, but that is not necessarily so. Flexibility is a function not of age but of personality. Contrary to the assumptions of some early psychologists, we now know that personality is not graven in stone at age five. People continue to develop and change throughout life.

Sarah Lowry had had a difficult life. She had raised her three children virtually alone because of her husband's chronic illnesses and need for prolonged hospitalizations. She felt estranged from her brother and sister, who, she thought, had gotten most of their parents' support and concern; since she was the eldest, nobody had thought she needed anything. Although her children and grandchildren lived in the same city, she felt that they were not really accessible to her. Now in her sixties, she was suffering from several chronic illnesses that restricted her freedom. Her doctor became concerned about her tendency to neglect necessary health care, and suggested she see a psychiatrist. This was rather a strange idea to Mrs. Lowry, but she thought highly of her doctor and agreed to see the person he recommended. Somewhat to her surprise, she found the psychiatrist easy to talk to. She found herself pouring out a lot of feelings she had never talked about before—especially anger.

Mrs. Lowry's income did not permit her to see the psychiatrist on a regular basis, so he referred her to a social work agency for which he was a consultant. Mrs. Lowry, once she had experienced the relief of talking about her feelings, was able to continue with another person. She saw the social worker for several months, and began to feel much more in control of her life. When her children noticed the change in her, she told them about the help she was getting. As a result, one of her sons decided to see a therapist. As mother and son each became more comfortable in reviewing their life experiences with their therapists, they were also able to share them with each other, and even with the other children in the family. Thus Mrs. Lowry's decision to seek help for herself created a benign spiral, which eventually made all the members of the family more accessible to each other because they were more comfortable with themselves.

Creating Second Chances: Finding Sources of Help

As Mrs. Lowry's experience illustrates, it is not necessary to shrug off feelings or avoid doing something about them at any age. Many potential facilitators of the process that helps with emotional growth exist, although finding the most appropriate one sometimes requires near-detective work.

There are many sources of help. Social work agencies have traditionally offered help in dealing with feelings as well as help in locating and mobilizing resources. Clergymen and physicians sometimes function as counselors. In addition, there are a host of therapists in private practice: psychiatrists, social workers, psychologists, specialists in family treatment, among others. But the variety of labels can be most confusing to someone who is in distress and casting about for help. It is useful to remember that the labels of these sources are less important than the effect of the help they can provide and the improvements in feelings and behavior that occur as a result. If one consults a potential helper and comes away feeling stronger, more hopeful, better able to cope, the connection has been useful. If, on the other hand, one feels more burdened, guilty, or confused, it is probably the wrong source of help, at least for that particular person. Credentials are useful in ascertaining what the helper's background and preparation have been, but, regardless of credentials, the proof of the value of help is in its effects on the quality of individual lives.

The most effective helper is one who can lead you to see something in your situation of which you were not already aware. Dr. David Gutmann of Northwestern University has provided a most succinct definition of the role of a therapist: "One who brings you news about yourself." The decision to consult someone usually occurs at a point of crisis. The Chinese word for "crisis" is composed of two characters, one meaning "danger," the other "opportunity." An effective therapist is one who can point out the opportunities as well as the dangers in one's personal crisis, and can identify ways of taking advantage of the potential gains as well as of dealing with the losses.

Peer Groups as Facilitators

In addition to the traditional one-to-one sources of help, there has been a great increase, in recent years, in the use of groups. People who share a common experience or problem can explore it together, and provide both support and new insights to each other.

A potential source of help to multi-generation families has been developed at the Continuum Center for Adult Counseling and Leadership Training, Rochester, Michigan.

Called "peer counseling," it involves teaching people to listen and respond to each other. In particular, it has been used with great success in many settings where elderly people congregate and seek an opportunity to share their concerns. It has thus made the therapeutic process available to more than those few who already have a natural aptitude for introspection.

Joseph Mandel is one of those who found in peer counseling a means of growth. He had always been an active man, and, when he retired, found the hours difficult to fill. He had never been a very articulate person, but in a group of other retired people he found it easier to talk. He found that they had similar frustrations and concerns. As they described their efforts to deal with these concerns, he felt encouraged to try new approaches himself.

One of his frustrations was that although he was very proud of his children, he did not feel close to them. He assumed that since he had had a blue-collar job all his life and they were "professionals," they would not be interested in his opinions or feelings. As he talked and listened to his peers, and began to understand their struggles to communicate with their children, he gained courage to try to express his feelings to his children, too. He was amazed and gratified to discover that they were also proud of him, and that not only they but his grandchildren were interested in hearing about his early life. It gave them a sense of having roots. Without the practice sessions provided by the peer-counseling group, Mr. Mandel and his family might never have learned to express their appreciation of each other.

The middle-aged, who so often feel caught in a squeeze play between the young and the old, can also use peer groups for mutual support and practical help. But group learning need not be confined to one generation. Members of different generations can enhance each other's perception of life. In recognition of this fact, at least one community college has actively recruited people of different ages (eighteen through eighty plus) to participate in its course on aging. As a result, the old people discovered that the young ones were not necessarily rude and selfish; the young people discovered that the old ones had much practical wisdom, humor, and interesting life experience. Both groups learned to value old age as a time of continuing learning, rather than fearing it as a time of loss and isolation.

The Advantages of Different Perspectives

The seminars and groups mentioned above are examples of the ways in which people of different ages can learn to enjoy each other, once they feel secure enough to stop competing and begin to listen. It bears out the saying (attributed to Mark Twain, among others): "When I was fourteen my father was the most stupid person I had ever met; but by the time I was twenty-one, I was amazed at how much he had learned in seven years."

Events change in their meaning for people at different stages of life. A traumatic event for a teenager—such as a misunderstanding at a school dance—may be chuckled over by the same person by the time he is forty, and remembered nostalgically at seventy.

Family resemblance is one of the constants which change in meaning. Children and adolescents are apt to be exasperated by any evidence that they look like their parents. It feels like a restriction, and an attempt to deny their uniqueness. For the middle-aged, such likenesses give a feeling of continuity, and for the old, they are the proof of immortality—the indestructibility of the self, the validation of uniqueness rather than the denial of it.

Interaction with others is the chief way in which we extend our own experience. Intergenerational contacts help us to become aware of what the future holds—and prepare us to deal with it more effectively. If the old and the young can sustain a dialogue and continue talking to each other, even about their differences, they will find in each other's faces both challenge and reassurance.

7

When to Worry—And What to Do About It

Always in the minds of the old and their families is the fear of deterioration to the point of helplessness. Frequently the assumption is that when, or if, it happens, there are only two choices: the family must saddle itself with the responsibility for twenty-four-hour care or "put Mother away." The dilemma is equally painful for the old person where the choices seem to be "becoming a burden" or facing the prospect of exile from the family, and this is compounded by the anticipated loss of freedom, dignity, and personhood which is conjured up by thoughts of entering a nursing home.

The reality is not so bleak. Institutionalization is not the only way to deal with deficits, and even when it is necessary, it need not mean loss of human contact. But before looking at the options it is important to ask some questions. When is a change in living arrangements necessary? What signs should be cause for anxiety and action? And who should take the action?

Distinguishing Inconvenience from Jeopardy

There can be no question that deterioration is frightening to watch. Forgetfulness, increasing frailty, progressive illness all stir up anxiety and a wish to protect the one suffering from such disabilities. The sufferer, however, may not want to be protected, and may, in fact, be coping very well despite his or her handicaps.

Clara Jenkins was in her eighties. She had sustained a broken hip, but recovered and insisted on returning to her own apartment. Although she had regained her mobility, she also suffered from a cardiac problem, which became progressively worse. Despite repeated hospitalizations, she was determined to stay out of a nursing home, and with the aid of her daughter, neighbors, and community services she managed. But as the years passed, and hospitalizations got closer and closer together, her daughter became increasingly anxious. Mother was likely to call her at any hour of the day or night. Although Clara Jenkins was very independent, not to say stubborn, she always became panicky when she was ill. Daughter tried to persuade Mrs. Jenkins to accept nursing-home care, but she insisted that she would die alone in her apartment rather than consider any such thing. Since she also made it clear that she did not want to die alone, her daughter felt caught between her mother's independent stance which alternated with cries for help, and her own sense of responsibility.

She confided all this to the social worker who had arranged for home health services. The worker reminded her that Mrs. Jenkins had a right to remain in her own home if she chose; that she was, in fact, doing quite well between acute episodes of illness; and that, in any case, she had always done exactly as she pleased and was not likely to change this pattern at eighty-seven. "I know, I know," the daughter sighed, "but how long can I stand to watch?"

Watching an elderly parent struggle against disability is indeed difficult. It feels different from watching a child strike out on his own, because even while we worry about the hazards, we anticipate that the child's judgment and skills will become equal to the task. We know that he cannot grow to adulthood without taking on risks. With an old person, we are more apt to think that he has nothing more to gain by continuing the struggle, since his physical disabilities are likely to get worse. Despite increasing frailty, however, many old people are by no means ready to give up. They could say, in the words of the old spiritual, "I'm a little sick, but I ain't noways tired." The security of total care does not appeal to them if it means loss of their freedom to act and control their lives. To quote Andrew Marvell again:

> The grave's a fine and private place,
> But none I think do there embrace.

The fears of those elderly who see institutional care as a living graveyard, and the anxieties of their families who must watch progressive deterioration, may create an impasse. What guidelines can be provided to help them determine the wisest course of action? What should be cause for concern, and what options are available? The rest of this chapter is an attempt to provide some answers.

The Limits of Risk-Taking

How much disability is too much? The answer to this really depends on two factors. The first is the nature of the disability and the extent to which it interferes with one's usual activities. The second is the nature and extent of the help available to compensate for the disability. Mr. Farley, for instance, may be rather vague about what day it is, but manages to provide quite adequately for his daily needs. If, however, his forgetfulness increases to the point where he gets lost on the way to the grocery store, or forgets to eat altogether, that is another story. On the other hand, Mrs. Smith may be a charming companion, a gracious hostess to all the neighborhood children, but if she cannot light the stove without burning herself, or regulate the medicines she must take to maintain her health, she is in trouble unless she can get help in performing these necessary tasks.

The availability of help is often the crucial factor in determining how much disability is tolerable. Perhaps Mr. Farley had been forgetful all along, but no one noticed it while his wife was living. She shopped, prepared the meals, and reminded him when it was time to eat. After she died, he had no one to structure his day and perhaps little reason to feel like eating. The loss of a caretaker changed his disability from a minor nuisance to a major hazard. If other supports can be provided to substitute for the loss to some extent—through family, neighbors, or community services—Mr. Farley may be able to continue life in his familiar surroundings. If not, he may have to face being uprooted in addition to his other losses, not because his disability is greater but because his support system is smaller.

When Disability Increases

Sometimes the deterioration itself progresses to the point where neither the individual nor the family can deal with it. When such a change occurs, the questions that need to be considered are not only "What care is available?" but "What treatment is possible?"

Maude Vance was eighty-one, and had been living alone since her husband died. She was an enthusiastic amateur painter, and also took ceramics lessons at a nearby center, where she made many friends. These activities came to a sudden halt when she suffered several fractures in an automobile accident. Although the bones healed, she was slow to regain her mobility and tired easily. It was too long a walk to the center, so she gave up going. Although both of her daughters lived in the same city and visited regularly, she spent much of her time at home alone.

One midnight she called the older daughter, in great agitation. "James didn't come home for supper, and I can't find my little ones," she sobbed. Puzzled, her daughter reminded Mrs. Vance that her "little ones" were grown-up, and that her husband had been dead for many years. Mrs. Vance was reassured momentarily, but the idea persisted. She called not only her daughters but also the police, and spent her afternoons searching through a nearby park for her "little ones."

Her daughters, bewildered and anxious, speculated that perhaps Mother had developed these bizarre ideas because she was alone too much. They thought she might be happier in a retirement home where she could have twenty-four hour care and companionship. The social worker who took the application, however, suggested a different approach. "This change has come about so suddenly," she said. "I think you need to find out what is causing it before taking any action."

"But she did see a doctor," one of the daughters objected. "He said it was hardening of the arteries."

"What sort of examination did he make?" the worker questioned.

"Oh, the usual, I suppose. He talked to her for about ten minutes. Actually, we answered most of the questions."

In further discussion, the daughters stated that the doctor

had seen Mrs. Vance only once, and had not ordered any additional tests.

The worker then suggested that Mrs. Vance could go to a diagnostic center specializing in the treatment and care of elderly people. There it could be determined whether a medically treatable condition was causing her problem. If not, the center could also make recommendations for further care, since they not only test for specific diseases but also observe the way the person responds to his environment.

Mrs. Vance spent a week at the diagnostic center. It was established that her problem was the result of several factors. A series of small strokes had indeed affected her memory to some extent. Nevertheless, her "delusions" about her husband and children were not due to her organic impairment itself, but were instead an emotional reaction, not only to the memory loss but to the loss of mobility, rewarding activities, and friendships which had been the result of her auto accident. As many people do through reminiscing, she had tried to recapture an earlier, more gratifying period of her life when her husband and babies needed her. Emotional pressure and organic deficit combined to blur the distinction for her between past and present, reality and memory. In her frantic searches through the park, she had mourned the earlier as well as the later losses.

The center's recommendation, like its diagnosis, was multiple. It included medication, structured activities, and readily available human contact. Mrs. Vance's medications were regulated and the family taught how to set them up in color-coded bottles so that it would be easier for her to take them at the correct times. A day-care center was found which could provide Mrs. Vance with companionship and activities, give her scope for her artistic skills, and monitor her diet and medications. The day-care center also offered daily transportation to and from the center, which provided a relief to the family, who took over on the weekends.

Mrs. Vance enjoyed the day-center program, resumed her painting, even gave lessons to some of the other users. Although she was still alone at night, her preoccupation with her lost "little ones" diminished and finally stopped altogether, as did her midnight calls to her daughters and the police. Although her organic deficits were about the same as before, she was able to enjoy her life once more, and manage much of it on her own.

The Importance of Complete Diagnosis

Mrs. Vance's story illustrates the importance of identifying all the factors involved when there is a change in an elderly person's ability to function. (It is, of course, important for everybody, but is most likely to be neglected in the old.) In Mrs. Vance's case, the initial diagnosis ("hardening of the arteries") was not so much incorrect as incomplete. It left the patient and her family with no information as to what, besides circulatory changes, was affecting her, or what could be done about it.

Many organic conditions besides hardening of the arteries can present symptoms of confusion, disorientation, and memory loss. Among them are undiagnosed heart attacks, diabetes, infections, tumors, and malnutrition. Early diagnosis is essential in determining whether such a treatable condition exists. If they are not caught early, such diseases can either kill the patient or result in irreversible brain damage.

When patients originally diagnosed as suffering from "chronic organic brain syndrome" were re-examined after they had spent several years in a state hospital for the mentally ill, 15 percent were found to have treatable illnesses. When the illnesses were treated, the confusion decreased or disappeared.[1] If 15 percent were still treatable after so long a time, how many could have been saved by earlier diagnosis!

Even when a specific, treatable condition exists, there are always other factors that affect the patient's ability to benefit by the treatment. His understanding or misconception about his illness, his confidence or fear, family support or lack of it, financial resources, and the availability of appropriate services all play a part, and need to be taken into account in determining both the cause of the disability and the treatment of choice.

Mrs. Vance was fortunate in having both a diagnostic center and community services available to her. Of course, not everyone has such resources available, although two diagnostic centers which specialize in the diagnosis and treatment of the elderly—the Philadelphia Geriatric Center in Philadelphia, and the Johnston R. Bowman Health Center for the Elderly in Chicago (see Appendix I, Medical Agencies, for addresses and referral information)—do accept patients from other parts of the country. But for those who must find their own answers locally, it may be helpful to know what the diagnostic centers look for, and how they use the information.

Taking Stock: The Diagnostic Center Model

The purpose of admission to a diagnostic center is to learn as much as possible about the old person's problem, as a means of determining what can best be done about it. The sources of information include medical, neurological, psychiatric, and psychological testing. Not all the possible tests are done for each individual, but the range of tools does exist. As the evaluation progresses, these methods are used to seek answers to the questions actually raised. Occupational and physical therapists also can assess the patient's environment and may recommend modifications that would make it easier for him to manage (i.e., raising the height of a toilet seat or eliminating scatter rugs or adding handrails in the bathtub area). Thus the intent is to augment the medical information with a detailed profile of the person's functioning in his home, in his family, and in his community. Relationships with family and friends are explored to determine what supports are available as well as what problems may be interfering with their use. Particular attention is paid to crisis points and recent changes in both health and social situation. When the evaluation is completed, the doctors and other involved staff present their findings and recommendations to the patient and his family. These include not only the current picture but also the prognosis. It is important for patient and family to know whether the condition is likely to be fairly stable, to deteriorate slowly or rapidly, or to be amenable to rehabilitation.

Taking Stock: Designing Your Own Model

Those who do not have access to a diagnostic center may have to utilize several different facilities to get their questions answered. The family doctor, the local hospital, other specialists, a family service agency in the community, or the social service department of a hospital, perhaps a senior citizens' club or other community group organized for the older persons, may all be able to provide a part of the answer. In using such a combination, it helps to have one's questions assembled in advance. The specifics, of course, will depend on the individual situation, but some general questions can help to pinpoint the nature of almost any problem. Among the most pertinent of these are:

> How long has the problem been in existence?
> What is different about it now? Why does it require attention now, if it didn't before?
> What changes have occurred recently in the patient's life?
> What significant event may have occurred in the past that the person is reacting to now (i.e., anniversary of the death of a loved one, an old anger reborn because of a current reminder, and so on)?
> Have there been any recent changes in the lives of family or friends (i.e., daughter's vacation trip, son's move to another town, the death of a peer or a relative)?
> If there are physical changes, what are they, and what do they mean? What treatment is required/possible?
> What can the person still do himself/herself? What does he/she need help in doing?
> What resources for treatment/assistance are available?

Too often, families in crisis ask only the last question (i.e., "How do I find a nursing home?" or "Do you have a recreation program?"). Asking about a specific solution only, without considering the other questions, is likely to result in a bewildering variety of answers, or none at all.

The Visible Infirmities: Potential for Rehabilitation

An important consideration, especially for victims of heart attacks, fractures, or strokes, is the potential for correction of the disability. Fatigue, poor balance, muscle weakness, slurred speech, or other residuals all may be correctable, at least to some extent, by prompt and adequate rehabilitative therapy. Many hospitals have rehabilitation units where such therapies are provided, or access to other hospitals or facilities that specialize in this kind of treatment. However, this is not true of all hospitals, and not all physicians think of the elderly as suitable candidates, particularly if they or their families do not press the issue. Because rehabilitation is most effective if begun as soon as possible after the damage has occurred, it is important to raise the question early. It may also be worthwhile to get a second opinion. As we saw with Margaret McClendon (page 53), the potential for recovery may be underestimated, and the patient's own determination has a great deal to do with the outcome.

Another difficulty especially for a patient with Parkinsonism or a stroke victim, is the fact that the person *looks* different. This will have an effect on family and friends and certainly on the patient as well. A drooping eyelid or drooling mouth, unsteady gait or dragging foot may be seen as a sign of greater disability than it actually is. It may be quite possible for a patient with muscle weakness to perform tasks such as dressing, or for one whose speech is affected to make himself or herself understood, given enough *time.* Even when the process of recovery seems to have come to a standstill, it is important to remember that the person inside the damaged body is still the same. He or she still needs not only care but the opportunity to exercise whatever skills he or she still possesses, as well as the opportunity to communicate and to be heard. It is difficult enough to have one's body refuse to respond to the mind's commands. If those around the one who is struggling against a handicap are in too much distress, or in too much hurry to slow their pace to the unsteady steps or the halting speech, it adds insult to injury.

A newspaper reporter recently wrote a poignant account of how she had set out eagerly to write an article about the plight of the handicapped, only to find herself impatient and uncomfortable when confronted by a man who was actually dealing with a handicap. His greatest frustration was that everybody was in too great a rush to wait for him to get his words out. The reporter, who was under pressure to get back to her office and write the article, asked him what would be of most help to the handicapped. She thought he would mention research or contributions to charity. Instead, he said, "Make contact." Then, with a wry smile, he added, "This hasn't been so bad, has it?"[2]

Human contact is just as essential to handicapped people as to "normal" ones, and just as essential to the old as to the young.

Evaluating the Evaluators

Old people and their families may need help not only in assessing the situation, altering their attitudes and behavior, or adjusting to new circumstances without immediately considering radical changes, but also in assessing the credentials and expertise of those from whom they seek advice and counsel. The question as to whether deterioration has progressed to the point where an alternative living arrangement or other help is necessary is one that is fraught with emotion. It usually arises at a time of crisis and trauma. Families are likely to have had no previous experience and little information that could guide them in weighing the issues. They need a basis for intelligent consumerism.

If a doctor says that Mama should be in a nursing home, should one take his word for it? If another doctor says she doesn't need one, which should the family believe? If one neighbor swears by the family helper and companion agency, and another swears *at* it, which of them is right?

How does one go about determining which piece of advice, and which service, is right for one's own situation?

Following are some general guidelines, as well as some "red flags" to keep in mind.

One may be better off with a doctor who has had a good deal of experience in treating the elderly, but this is not universally true, for experience can be used to confirm one's prejudices rather than to expand one's horizons. More important than experience is willingness to learn, to keep abreast of new developments, to be unafraid to say "I don't know. . . . I'll try to find out." A doctor should be able to explain his diagnosis in terms of how it affects the patient, what changes in his routine it is likely to require, and what danger signs, if any, should be watched for. For instance, a diabetic needs to know that the disease affects his body's ability to use sugar, that the recommended diet or medication is to compensate for the lack, and that other systems of the body may be affected as well. Therefore symptoms that seem unrelated, such as changes in vision or sores on the foot, should be reported immediately.

A doctor should also be able to explain the basis for his recommendation, whether that recommendation concerns surgery, medical treatment, or institutional care. If he says a nursing home is needed, ask him why. What care will the home provide, and what hazards will it prevent? Are there other possibilities for accomplishing what is needed?

It is always legitimate to ask for an explanation of the diagnosis and recommendations, as well as to ask for a second opinion. No competent physician will be insulted by such a request; indeed, he may suggest it before the patient does.

Although the physician should be able to describe and

justify his recommendations for care, he may not be familiar with the range of methods for providing care. If one needs to know what, besides a nursing home, might be utilized, the question may be better addressed to a social service agency, either in the hospital or in the community. Most social workers are knowledgeable about community resources. Since not only the medical recommendations but emotional, family, and financial considerations have a bearing on the decision to be made, social workers can help families to get a clearer understanding of the total situation and to reflect on the appropriateness of any plan in the light of all that is known about the older person and his circumstances. Just receiving nursing-home information without first getting a sense of what the specific individual and family needs are is not likely to constitute good advice. One could do as well in the yellow pages of telephone directories. In other words, the object is to obtain a tailor-made solution and not be content with a list of names.

Social workers, like doctors or any other professionals, should be able to explain the basis for their recommendations. Neither social workers nor doctors are miracle workers or mind readers, however. They cannot locate what does not exist, or answer questions that have not been asked.

Some attitudes give warning of trouble. The professional who is "too busy" to explain or who seems bored and impatient should be avoided if possible. So should the one who says, "At your age, what does it matter?" or who suggests the same solution for everybody, or considers the situation too hopeless to bother about.

A son took his father to a clinic because the old man had been showing signs of confusion and also seemed to be neglecting his diet, eating nothing but sweets. The doctor who examined him was unconcerned about possible malnutrition. "Your father is senile," he stated flatly. "If he starves to death, it would be the best thing that could happen, for all of you." Unfortunately there are doctors, and social agencies as well, who consider it a waste of time to work with the elderly, even if they do not express their opinion so blatantly. When confronted by such an attitude, run, do not walk, to the nearest exit.

It must be remembered, however, that even when good professional experts are found, they can only augment a family's understanding of their situation. They cannot substitute for it, nor can they make the necessary decisions. Only the people directly involved can do that, for they will have to live with the decisions once they are made.

The limitations of relying on "expert" opinion are illustrated by a story remembered affectionately by students of Suzanne Schultze, a social work professor at the University of Chicago. Her class had been studying foster care and were considering the case of a small boy who was placed in a foster home just before the family went on vacation. As a result, the child had to cope with a whole series of changes rather than just the move to the foster home. Professor Schultze asked the class what they thought of the timing of the placement. One student defended it on the grounds that "the psychiatrist said he should be placed immediately." The professor straightened up in her chair, eyes flashing. "Well!" she snapped. "And is that the voice of God speaking?"

Professional opinion can be a valuable adjunct, a help and support in the decision-making process, but it does not negate what you already know about yourself and your family, nor should it minimize your ability to trust what feels right to you. A true test in arriving at a plan is the degree of comfort with which you, and all concerned, can accept it and act on it.

When More Care Is Needed: Range of Options

Suppose everyone is in agreement that Mama and (or) Papa need more help than they can provide for themselves. What are the possibilities?

COMBINING HOUSEHOLDS

One possibility, of course, is combining households. This was the usual solution—at least according to popular mythology—in an earlier America. There were, and are, advantages and disadvantages. Having older and younger families under one roof can ease financial pressure on both generations, and make all the members more readily available to each other for mutual assistance. On the other hand, it can interfere with everyone's needs for privacy and personal space, or lay an intolerably heavy burden of nursing care and service on one person, usually the daughter or daughter-in-law. Combined households probably work best when the parties to the arrangement are friends as well as relatives, when their life styles are reasonably compatible and/or enough space is available for everyone, and when the care-giving is mutual. In many families, for instance, Grandmother takes care of the children while both parents hold jobs outside the home. This may work out very well as long as Grandmother remains healthy. If Grandmother suffers some catastrophic illness that destroys the mutuality of the arrangement, the family may be forced to find alternative means of providing care not only for Grandmother

but for the children as well. The problems they then encounter are not the result of combined households, but of
loss of mutuality.

Introducing a newcomer to an existing household always
creates changes and dislocations. This is true whether the
addition is an infant or a grandparent, a foster child or a
new spouse, even a new pet. If one is considering such a
plan, it is a good idea to discuss beforehand the purposes
to be served by the move, and what it will mean for everybody.

Perhaps the proposal is to have Grandmother move into
the third bedroom, which is now occupied by Junior and
his train set. Is the purpose to relieve a financial crunch?
To provide nursing care for Grandmother? To provide a
baby-sitter for Junior? What will happen to Junior and his
trains? Will he move in with his brother (whose passion is
rock music) or will Mother and Father move to the couch
in the living room? Can Grandmother stand the rock music?
Can she get up and down stairs, or will she be confined
to her room? If Grandmother needs care, can it be provided
by the family without keeping anybody up day and night?
If she wants to help with household tasks, can the younger
members of the family accept such help? (The Chinese syn-
onym for "discord" is "two women under one roof.")

A family may take a grandparent or other relative into
its home in response to a crisis, and then be dismayed by
unforeseen problems. It is preferable to delay such a move
until the advantages and disadvantages have been thoroughly examined, and available alternatives considered. If
that is not possible, the move may be presented as a temporary measure to allow the total family, including the aged
relative, time to arrive at a more satisfactory plan.

Despite some disadvantages, the family may conclude

that combining households is the most feasible arrangement for their situation. If so, it is important to talk openly about what will be expected of everybody, including the newcomer. Having an opportunity to anticipate the changes, to state objections and suggest compromises, makes the adjustment easier. Even children can accept change more gracefully if they are involved in the advance planning, rather than confronted after the fact. It is also important to remember the distinction between talk and action. If the children and the adults, including Grandmother, can voice their objections openly and get a sympathetic hearing, they are less likely to act them out afterward. Repressive comments, such as "You mustn't talk like that about your grandmother," or "You should be grateful we can do this for you," are far more apt to result in anger (and possible sabotage of unspoken agreements) than open sharing of grievances ever would.

COMMUNITY SERVICES TO MAINTAIN SEPARATE HOUSEHOLDS

When older and younger families prefer to maintain separate households, they may seek community services to provide help for the elderly who live independently. To find appropriate help, it is useful to know what sorts of services may exist. Following are some of the more commonly available forms of help.

In-Home Help. Homemakers, housekeepers, or companions may perform such household tasks as cooking, shopping, laundry, and light housework. They may also be able to offer some supervision of the older person and assistance with personal care, such as bathing or dressing, accompanying on walks, and helping to maintain a medication schedule. Such helping personnel can usually be located through domestic employment agencies and are sometimes available through family service or social welfare agencies. Those provided by employment agencies are likely to be expensive. A subsidy may be available for those supplied by social service agencies. Other sources of supply may be the local college where students sometimes seek mother's-helper or live-in jobs either in exchange for room and board or as hourly work. High-school students may also be available for chores and errands. Mothers of school-age children may welcome the opportunity for a few hours of work while the children are away from home. The P.T.A. is a possible source of recruitment, as are community centers, churches, synagogues, and even the local grocery store. If you tell enough different people what you are looking for, word of mouth may lead you to the right person. Perhaps your son's best friend's Aunt Minnie has a daughter-in-law whose sister's girl is looking for an after-school job, and who would be willing to help Grandmother with shopping or other chores. Even in these days of computers, the neighborhood network should not be overlooked.

Nutrition Programs. When the older person is not homebound, but may find food preparation difficult or uninspiring, there may be community centers which serve nutritious meals at modest cost. For times of illness or recuperation, or if the older person is homebound for ongoing reasons, many localities now offer Meals on Wheels delivered directly to the home of the disabled person at mealtimes. The local area agency on aging or the state department on aging would be the best sources for locating such programs.

Transportation. Besides the public transportation discounts that exist in many cities, there are some programs that provide door-to-door pickup service for elderly people.

Where these programs exist, they may be limited to a single purpose, such as shopping or medical visits. For disabled persons, some private transportation companies have devised special buses that accommodate wheelchairs or other orthopedic appliances. This service is less expensive than a private ambulance, but more expensive than a taxi.

Home-Centered Health Services. A recent addition to the availability of care at home has been the burgeoning of home health agencies funded by Medicare. These provide not only the professional services of a nurse, physician, or physical therapist, but also assistance with bathing, dressing, shopping, household maintenance, and other services necessary to support an elderly person's convalescence at home. The services of a home health agency must be ordered and supervised by a physician. The chief limitation of such agencies is that they are designed for short-term illnesses that respond quickly to treatment. They do not provide for the chronically ill, or for those who need personal assistance but no skilled professional care. Nevertheless, home health care has made it possible for many people to recover from fractures, strokes, heart attacks, or other acute illnesses at home rather than in a nursing home. They have thus prevented many premature institutionalizations, especially for those who would not be able to pay for even temporary nursing-home care and still maintain their homes in the community.

Day Care. Centers providing care for the children of working mothers have long been in existence. Recently, the idea has been expanded to include day services for old people. These programs are designed for those who are physically or psychologically disabled enough to need some assistance and supervision during the day, but who are well enough to tolerate the trip back and forth. For the most part, the centers are used by people who are living alone, or whose families are not at home in the daytime. They provide not only care but activities, stimulation, and interaction with other people. For this reason, such programs may be preferable to staying at home with a companion.

THE NEED FOR COORDINATED SERVICES

Although many services exist, their distribution is very uneven. One community may have homemaker services; another, transportation to doctors; another, volunteer shoppers. Cities are generally better supplied than rural areas, but the variety of offerings may make a specific service more difficult to locate, or may require the use of several different agencies to secure the right combination. Success in finding what is needed often takes ingenuity, persistence, and luck. This lack of consistency and connection between services is a serious deterrent to their use, and a great source of frustration and discouragement to families and individuals who are seeking help.

In some places, public and private agencies are trying to devise a better system. The Council for Jewish Elderly in Chicago was set up in 1972 as a network of comprehensive and coordinated services, of which people could use one or many, and where they could move in and out of the system as their needs changed. Someone might need housekeeping help most of the time, add home-delivered meals or shopping assistance in the winter, and perhaps need no services at all during periods of better health. Several states have also begun to experiment with the idea of offering a cluster of services through one agency. If the idea catches on, and is emulated in other parts of the country, finding appropriate services will become very much easier for old people and their families.

INSTITUTIONAL SETTINGS

Sometimes no amount of service at home is effective, or the service that might be effective is unavailable. Those who need care may then have to consider the use of an institution. Obviously, this decision must be made by the old person and no discussion of such plans should bypass him or her.

The range of care available in institutions is almost as great as the range of services in the community. There are retirement homes and hotels that provide meals, housekeeping, and activities programs, but no medical supervision. Other group or "shelter care" homes dispense medicines and provide some assistance with bathing or other personal care. Nursing homes provide various levels of care, ranging from personal assistance to complex nursing and rehabilitation services. Finding the right setting for one's specific needs can be a formidable task. It involves not only recognizing the needs but assessing how well a particular institution is likely to meet them.

How to Recognize Good Institutional Care. The first step in recognizing good institutional care, as in recognizing quality in any other service, is knowing what you need. Perhaps Uncle Dick is independent in most respects but needs help in maintaining a complicated medication schedule. A skilled nursing facility would insure that he got his medicines at the proper time, but he might not be free to attend his beloved baseball games, and the other residents of the home might be too sick or confused to provide him with much companionship. No matter how good the nursing care provided, it would not meet Uncle Dick's needs. On the other hand, a retirement hotel which provides no medical supervision would leave him vulnerable to the dangers of undermedication or overmedication. Perhaps his medicines could be organized so that he could take them himself, or perhaps a different, less restrictive home could be found.

Families are often impressed by the newness of a home they are considering, but what pleases the family may not please the potential resident. One such family thought they had found the perfect solution for their grandmother in a glamorous-looking retirement hotel which provided meals and social activities in a pleasant suburban neighborhood. Grandmother, however, turned up her nose. *"Treif!"* was her verdict. The food was "not kosher" and none of the residents spoke Yiddish. She decided on a smaller and shabbier establishment that had these amenities, even though the neighborhood wasn't so nice.

It is ironic that the same families who want the newest for Grandma may make a different choice when considering their own needs. A residence for temporary care was housed in a rather shabby and run-down hotel, although the facility itself was attractive and homelike. Family members responding to a questionnaire on the use of the residence often stated that they would not use it for their parents. Yet the same people answered "yes" to the question "Would you use it yourself?"

Suppose you have identified the needs and found an institution that claims to meet them. How can you tell whether it will actually do so?

One index to quality of care is the patient-staff ratio. There should be enough staff so families do not feel the need to supplement, either with themselves or by hiring additional private-duty help. It is worthwhile to know what professional staff are available, and what shifts are covered. An R.N. may be in charge during the day shift, but who takes charge in the evening and at night? Is there a doctor on call, or does each patient supply his own? Under what circumstances would a doctor be called, or the patient sent to the hospital? If the administrator of the home is vague about any of these matters, that is a danger sign. One should also be wary if the administrator, or the director of nursing, is seldom available. Absentee management is a poor way to guarantee quality control.

The administrator should be willing to show all parts of the home, including the floors where confused or seriously ill patients are cared for. As you walk through the home, notice the attitude of the administrator to patients and staff. Is it friendly? Patronizing? Brusque? Indifferent? Does the administrator know the names of patients, or residents, and speak to them? The attitude of the staff is likely to reflect that of the administrator.

In touring a prospective home, you can observe much about the attitudes of the staff. Do they seem relaxed and friendly or rushed and irritable? You can also deduce a good deal about the home from the way the patients look. Are they dressed and well-groomed, or unkempt and in night clothes? Do they communicate with each other, or do they seem morose and withdrawn? Is there evidence of activities going on, or does everyone sit comatose in front of the television set?

The administrator should be able to describe the program of the home, including social activities and facilities for reha- bilitation, if any. Specialized staff, such as activity directors, physical therapists, or social workers, are often part-time employees. It is worthwhile to know how many days a week they spend at the home and what space and equipment they have to work with. The importance of their function in the overall scheme of things can often be deduced from such items. If the physical therapist is only there one day a week, and is alloted a poorly lit corner of a basement storage area, one may assume that his presence has little impact on the lives of most of the residents.

Most people who are examining an institution take note of housekeeping standards—whether the place looks and smells clean—but few think of asking to see the kitchen. Yet the sanitary standards and quality of food have a major effect on the health and satisfaction of the residents. Sample menus should be available for inspection. One can ask how these are developed, and what provision is made for special diets. Does the home have a staff dietitian or regular consultant? The times at which meals are served is also important to know. Some homes do not provide any food between 4:30 or 5:00 in the afternoon and 8:00 the next morning. Others serve an evening snack of some kind. Visiting at mealtimes can give an indication of whether the sample menus reflect what is actually served, as well as how attractively it is presented. Knowing someone who lives in the home or has had experience with it can provide one with additional information.

The administrator should give clear and frank information on financial matters, including basic costs, extras, and whether the home accepts public assistance subsidies. Indeed, one of the best indicators of quality is the administrator's willingness to answer not only financial questions but any question about patient care.

Sometimes the questions do not get asked. This may happen because potential users or their families do not know what to ask, or because, under the pressure of crisis, they are afraid of being rejected if they appear too fussy. For this reason it would be well to look into the question of institutional care before the crisis becomes imminent. One could then get an idea of what exists, the process of application, the likelihood of space being available when needed, or the existence of waiting lists. Unfortunately, many people are as loath to think about institutions as they are to make wills. There may be a superstitious fear that raising the question will precipitate the need. However, it costs nothing to inquire, and if the information is never needed, so much the better. Perhaps a relative or friend will benefit by one's curiosity. Only five percent of the elderly population are ever institutionalized, but the quality of life for those who make up that group is important to them and to their families.

Emotional Needs of the Institutionalized Impaired. In considering questions of cost, availability, and appropriate medical care, it is easy to forget that residents of institutions are still people with the same emotional needs as everyone else. Easiest of all to forget are the needs of "confused" people. If someone cannot remember what day it is or makes comments that sound bizarre, we tend to discount both their remaining abilities and their feelings. This may be a grave injustice.

Joe Lamon, at eighty-five, was considered rather strange by his neighbors. He was convinced that "little people" came into his apartment by way of the water pipes. He had harbored this idea ever since his wife died, and it was probably his way of providing himself with company. He had always been something of a "loner," and was, besides, extremely hard of hearing. If Joe had had a family, they might have thought his deficits made him a candidate for institutional care. As it was, he managed his daily affairs quite well. His chief difficulty was getting information from his doctors. He had to have things explained to him, very slowly, in a loud voice. Usually the speaker had to repeat his statements several times before Joe understood. Many doctors avoided trying to tell Joe anything because it took so long. They rationalized that he was probably too confused to understand. One who took the time, however, found Joe an intelligent and cooperative patient, who followed instructions faithfully.

Those who cannot maintain their daily routines, as Joe did, may have other skills. Mary Starr, for instance, was placed in a nursing home because she couldn't remember to turn her stove off and frequently let the bathtub overflow. Yet she played the piano beautifully. On one occasion, when a planned entertainment was cancelled, she played a full hour's recital of classical and popular music, entirely from memory.

Even those whose mental impairment is so extensive that they cannot find their rooms, do not remember whether they have eaten lunch, or perhaps do not recognize their own families, have responded to opportunities for creativity. Singing, painting, writing poetry, even dance and yoga have been engaged in by people whose physical and mental disabilities might be assumed to make such activities impossible. A whole range of art therapies is being developed to help people express themselves in ways other than "rational" speech. Some of the therapists have taken their cues from cultures that put less stress on rational discourse and more on emotional interaction and physical well-being. Perhaps we will discover that "senility" is a disease of Western civilization. It may not be such a disability in societies that are accustomed to "nonrational" modes of expression. The enthusiasm of many young people for Zen, yoga, and other disciplines from the East may eventually prove to be of great benefit to their grandparents!

Those who provide day-to-day care have the greatest opportunity for relating to the emotional needs of their charges. It is unfortunate that most nursing- and residential-care workers have had little preparation for dealing with people who cannot express their needs verbally. Until recently, there has not been much training available for such a task. Patients have been moved through their daily routines with varying degrees of thoroughness and as much dedication as their caretakers could muster. Even basic comfort—keeping people clean, dry, and fed—may be neglected when patients are undemanding or the job provides little incentive. On the other hand, agitation, screaming, or angry behavior may be ignored, dismissed as evidence of "senility," or controlled with drugs. No effort is made to understand the reason for such behavior, on the assumption that once the patient is diagnosed as "senile," there is nothing to understand.

A very different attitude results if staff members believe that even nonverbal behavior is purposeful and meant to communicate something. For instance, Mrs. Coles picked up a newspaper and threw it after she was reprimanded by a nurse for some infraction of rules. The nurse reported to her supervisor that Mrs. Coles was "violent." Instead of taking the nurse's word for it, the supervisor went to Mrs. Coles and asked her why she threw the newspaper. Mrs. Coles pointed out that she hadn't thrown it *at* anybody, and the floor wasn't hurt. She was angry about being scolded and "treated like a child." The supervisor then reassured her staff that Mrs. Coles was neither unrealistic nor out of control. In addition to providing Mrs. Coles with a sympathetic ear, the supervisor had given the nursing staff an example of respect and concern for patients. Examples are much more impressive than words, and supervisory or administrative attitude and example set the tone for staff-patient interaction.

The needs and frustrations of both nurses and patients are suggested by the following poem which was found among the effects of a patient who had died in the Oxford University Geriatric Service facility in England. The author is unknown.

What Do You See?

What do you see, nurses? What do you see—
Are you thinking, when you are looking at me:
A crabbit old woman, not very wise,
Uncertain of habit, with faraway eyes,
Who dribbles her food, and makes no reply,
When you say in a loud voice, "I do wish you'd try."
Who seems not to notice the things that you do,
And forever is losing a stocking or shoe;
Who unresisting or not lets you do as you will,
When bathing and feeding, the long day to fill.
Is that what you are thinking, is that what you see?
THEN OPEN YOUR EYES, NURSES,
YOU ARE NOT LOOKING AT ME.

I'll tell you who I am, as I sit here so still,
As I rise at your bidding, as I eat at your will.
I'm a small child of ten, with a father and mother,
Brothers and sisters, who love one another;
A young girl of sixteen, with wings on her feet,
Dreaming that soon now a lover she'll meet;
A bride soon at twenty, my heart gives a leap,
Remembering the vows that I promised to keep;
At twenty-five now, I have young of my own,
Who need me to build a secure happy home;
A woman of thirty, my young now grow fast,

Bound to each other, with ties that should last;
At forty my young sons now grow and will be all gone,
But my man stays beside me, to see I don't mourn;
At fifty, once more babies play round my knee,
Again we know children, my loved one and me.

Dark days are upon me, my husband is dead.
I look at the future, I shudder with dread.
For my young are all busy, rearing young of their own,
And I think of the years, and the love that I've known.
I'm an old woman now, and nature is cruel.
It's her jest, to make old age look like a fool.
The body it crumbles, grace and vigour depart,
There is now a stone, where I once had a heart.
But inside this old carcass, a young girl still dwells,
And now and again, my battered heart swells;
I remember the joy, I remember the pain,
And I'm loving and living life all over again.
I think of the years, all too few—gone too fast,
And accept the stark fact that nothing can last.
So open your eyes, nurses, open and see
Not a crabbit old woman. Look closer—see ME.

Some homes have developed ways of helping their staff
to see the impaired person as an individual with needs and
wants, rather than as an unpleasant vegetable to be maintained. One of these is the Baycrest Centre for Geriatric
Care in Toronto, Canada, which has offered a training program in dealing with confused patients to staff of thirty-
four homes for the aged in Ontario. They have learned,
by careful observation, to understand from residents' actions what they need and want, even if they cannot communicate it verbally. For instance, one resident habitually
screamed and sang bawdy songs at bathtime. The nurse
decided that the lady was embarrassed at having to be un-
dressed in front of orderlies who lifted her in and out of

the tub. She assured the patient that she would always be covered when the two orderlies were present, and saw to it that this was done. The lady stopped screaming.[3]

Families as well as staff members may be intimidated by the behavior of those diagnosed as mentally impaired. Yet their behavior may be no different in meaning from what it was before the diagnosis.

Mr. Rand, who was accustomed to having his wife wait on him, was very upset when she had cataract surgery and needed care herself. When they were admitted to a home for the duration of her convalescence, he became very difficult to manage, threatening to walk out unless he got attention from his wife. Mrs. Rand was frantic. It was all due to his "chronic brain syndrome," she told the nurses. The floor nurse was not perturbed. "Syndrome, shmindrome," she replied, "he's having a tantrum." She told Mr. Rand, cheerfully but firmly, that it was not time for him to go home yet, and found some other activities to keep him occupied. Mr. Rand relaxed and settled down. He seemed reassured by having someone in charge who knew what he needed and was not afraid of him.

To Move or Not to Move. It is much easier to describe the ideal setting than to find it. If an old person is living in a less than ideal institution, should he or his family try to find another? Sometimes a move, if it can be arranged, is very beneficial. When staff members are indifferent or abusive, when needed therapeutic or social activities are unavailable, or when the level of care is unsuited to the patient's needs, it makes sense to look for a place that corrects these deficiencies.

A move is often advisable if the patient needs either more care or less care than his present location is providing. Hilda Van Zant, for instance, had originally gone into a nursing home to recuperate from a fracture. Since she had not been able to pay for both the nursing home and the rent on her apartment, she gave up the apartment. After the fracture healed, she had no place to go, so she stayed in the nursing home. She made herself useful to the other residents, and functioned almost like a staff member. Five years later a "commune" for elderly people opened, in which the residents took care of their own personal needs but had staff help for the heavier housekeeping, cooking, and maintenance chores. Mrs. Van Zant applied and was accepted. She became a leader among the residents of the commune, took swimming lessons, sewed for charity, and baby-sat for the children across the street. The commune was obviously much more compatible with her abilities than the nursing home had been.

The problem may not be the amount but the quality of care, as illustrated by the experience of the Spencers. Mr. Spencer first placed his wife in a nursing home that was only a few blocks from his apartment, so that he could visit her daily. As time passed, however, he became more and more displeased with the care she was receiving. The aides shouted at Mrs. Spencer and shoved her when she did not move quickly enough to suit them. More than once, her husband found her tied to her chair, or lying on her bed wet and filthy. After numerous protests to the administrator, Mr. Spencer decided to move his wife to another home. The one he chose was further away and he could only get there twice a week. But the quality of care was much more satisfactory. Mr. Spencer had made the difficult choice between seeing his wife more often and insuring that she was getting good treatment when he was not there.

Making one move may indeed result in better care. But sometimes families make a whole series of moves in an attempt to find the "perfect" solution. Not only is this a futile effort, but the repeated dislocations interfere with the old person's ability to cope, and may hasten his deterioration. Changes are difficult at any age; they are particularly hard for those whose physical and mental functioning are on the decline. For this reason it is important for families to weigh the possible benefits of a move against the difficulties of accommodating to a new location. If a move seems advisable, it helps to draw up a list of all the improvements one would like to see, and try to find as many as possible in one setting. It is easy to suppose that any change must be for the better, but, all too often, a move solves one problem and creates three others.

Families sometimes resort to moving as a means of dealing with guilt. Distressed by the deterioration that is occurring, they feel that as long as they are scurrying about, pulling strings, and making arrangements, they are "doing something" about the condition itself. This sensation of movement may be comforting for the family, but deleterious for the old person. It may help the family to remember that *it is not their fault* that one of their members is sick, whether that member is a parent, spouse, or child.

Preparation for a Move. Some of the adverse effects of a move may be avoided by sufficient preparation. If the person for whom care is being sought is involved in the decision-making, the move will be both less traumatic and less likely to be sabotaged. Families are sometimes reluctant to involve the care-needing member (old or young) because "it will upset him" or "he won't understand." The disabled person may be upset initially, but it is better for him to know what is happening and to express his objections. If he does not have this opportunity, he will certainly feel betrayed and abandoned if he is placed in an institution or moved to another without warning. Such feelings are likely to make him uncooperative and withdrawn, and may well negate the benefits of the placement.

Involving the person who needs care may be most difficult if he is extremely forgetful and confused. Telling him very much in advance may worry him because he cannot retain the information but feels that "something is happening." For such a one, it is better to tell him about the move very close to the time it is to be implemented, to stay with him during the transition, and to make frequent visits during the first few weeks after the move. A confused person who has experienced a move may be agitated and angry in the beginning. What can reassure him the most is his family's presence, and their confidence that the move is a good one. If they are uneasy and doubtful, the patient will be, too. For this reason, the family may want to get professional consultation, for their own reassurance, before going ahead with a move.

WHEN THE PERSON IN JEOPARDY REFUSES HELP: PROTECTIVE SERVICES

Families experience great anxiety and frustration when an elderly relative appears to be in real trouble but insists he is doing fine and refuses all offers of help. What can be done in such a situation?

Social service agencies receive many calls from relatives and others concerned about isolated or neglected old people. Although the caller may be unnecessarily anxious, the concern is often quite justified. Someone who is wandering, suffering frequent falls, living in filthy and dangerous surroundings without sufficient food or medical care is certainly at risk and in need of attention. To seek professional help for him is most appropriate, even though it may be difficult to get him to accept it. Having access to a trained opinion can help the family or other concerned people to determine how bad the situation really is. If it turns out that the person is eccentric, perhaps troublesome, but not really in jeopardy, that in itself can be reassuring to the family. Sometimes the elderly person, even though he has rejected the family's efforts to intervene, will welcome the attention of an outsider and, in time may agree to accept some service that would increase his safety and comfort. The more disabled a person is, the more he is likely to dread losing control of his life. If the social worker or other involved outsider can help him to see that getting service need not deprive him of all control, he may be relieved and grateful to take it.

But sometimes no amount of persuasion is effective, and the person is in real danger. What then? In that case the family may have to resort to legal remedies, and will need both legal and medical consultation. A court hearing may determine that the person is incompetent to manage his affairs, or that he is mentally ill. A guardian or conservator may then be appointed, or the person may be committed to a hospital. Measures of this kind are often difficult to put into effect, and the family—if any—may be reluctant to take legal proceedings because they don't want to subject their relative to the "stigma" of incompetency, or because they fear community criticism. There are times, however, when there is really no other means of getting a severely impaired person out of a dangerous situation. To do nothing can only result in further neglect, perhaps danger, not only to the well-being of the person himself but also to that of others. Someone who forgets to turn off the gas, for instance, or tries to heat his apartment by burning old newspapers, creates a hazard for his neighbors as well as himself.

Miss Rizzo, an isolated eighty-eight-year-old woman who had always been somewhat suspicious, became convinced that she was the victim of a conspiracy. She believed that the university near which she lived was going to kidnap her and "cut her up for research." To prevent this, she took to sitting up all night, and stopped taking her medicines. As a result, her health got worse. She started showing signs of dehydration and heart decompensation. She refused to let anyone into her apartment, and threw her shoes at the mailman. Her only close relative, a niece, tried to get her to "be reasonable," but the old lady would have nothing to do with her. In desperation, the niece resorted to commitment proceedings, and the police removed Miss Rizzo to a hospital. The following day the niece, in great trepidation, went to visit her aunt. She found her clean, fed, and looking much better than she had in the apartment. "My dear," said Miss Rizzo with her usual sternness, "I don't know what you could have been thinking of, to send me to a place like this . . . unless you were concerned for my safety!" Even the most vigorous protester is often relieved when someone takes charge and protective measures are taken.

The Frustration of Inadequate Services

Despite one's best efforts to secure them, the services needed by an elderly person may be unavailable or inadequate. It is extremely frustrating to know that hot meals or housekeeping help might be enough to let Mother stay in her own home, and not to be able to get them. It is equally frustrating to know that good institutional care exists, and to be unable to find it. Families who have to make do with less than the best for their aged members get angry. So they should—it is inexcusable that the richest country in the world should provide so shabbily for those who have spent a lifetime contributing to its welfare. It is far better that the old people, and their families, should be angry at not getting what they need than that they should feel guilty for needing it. If they are vociferous enough, an adequate service network may yet be developed.

In 1900, people over sixty-five made up 4 percent of the population. In 1970, this figure had grown to 10 percent. And the numbers are still mounting, as better health care results in longer life, and lower birth rates tip the population balance in favor of the old.

One advantage of these changes is a vast increase in community services designed for elderly people. Just as the baby boom of the 1940s produced a wave of schools and suburbs, so the geriatric population explosion is creating a proliferation of senior centers, nutrition programs, and home health agencies. These are, in fact, only a few of the most popular and visible services. Others, for which the demand is usually greater than the supply, are transportation, Meals on Wheels, and various kinds of household help.

The benefits of the geriatric population explosion may not come soon enough to serve all the members of the present generation of old people, but they should give reason for their children and their children's children to face the future with more hope than dread.

8

When It's Time to Say Goodbye

Whether one's life has been satisfying or frustrating, sooner or later the fact must be faced that it will end. This comes as a surprise to every individual, for, despite all human experience to the contrary, we tend to live as if we had unlimited time until something happens to remind us differently. Then we must deal with these questions. What has been accomplished? What has it been worth? What can be preserved and conveyed to others? The "something" that triggers such stocktaking may be a death in one's peer group, a move to a "protective" setting, the "sudden" adulthood of the young, or, perhaps, the inescapable awareness of physical enfeeblement. Once the recognition occurs, how does one deal with it? How do we prepare for the unexpected but inevitable end?

Other lands, other centuries have had their rituals of preparation, which perhaps eased the way. "Remember, oh man, that thou art dust . . ." declares the ancient Ash Wednesday ceremony. Douglas Steere tells of the Norwegian farmer who, in the fall before the roads became impassable, selected a coffin and took it home in case he should need it that winter.[1] Such activities seem strange, even morbid, to most twentieth-century Americans. Perhaps our romance with technology has made us believe that death is not an inevitable part of the life cycle, but a failure of the system, a regrettable lapse for which somebody must be to blame. Under that assumption, preparation is neither permissible nor possible. Such an unrealistic attitude puts us in a terrible bind. Denying death, we treat whole areas of life as if they did not exist.

Aging, which culminates in death, tends to be feared and avoided like the harbinger of plague. The aging who stay healthy may be pointed out as admirable exceptions, but signs of deterioration strike fear in the hearts of both the affected person and his loved ones, and conjure up images of helplessness, isolation, pain, and all the indignities of an animal existence in the back wards of some nursing home or hospital.

Not only the aging, but those diagnosed as terminally ill, whatever their age, are shunned. Their friends don't know how to talk to them; their doctors don't want to treat them; Medicare and other insurance won't cover the cost of their care. They are apt to be spoken of, even in their presence, as if they no longer had feelings or opinions. The focus tends to be on the illness, not on the person who is suffering from it. It is perhaps no wonder that the dying pick up the feeling that they must be at fault—like the man who referred to the failure of chemotherapy to control his cancer as "flunking his chemistry exam."

Not only the dying but also the bereaved are the victims of this universal phobia. Although those who have lost a loved one are usually treated with sympathy and tangible marks of concern, there is almost a conspiracy of silence in regard to the loss itself and its meaning to them. Uncertain as to what to say, fearful of being intrusive or burdensome, most people avoid the subject altogether. Those in mourning are thus likely to be treated as fragile and untouchable—in a word, taboo.

Much of the fear associated with death is probably due to the way society treats these three groups—those expected to die, those actually dying, and those who mourn. The Norwegian farmer, in preparing for the eventuality of his death in a practical and direct manner, eased the way for himself and those around him. He knew, after all, that however death came upon him, he would not have to face it in unfamiliar surroundings, separated from friends and family. He also knew that he would continue to be treated as himself, without loss of identity or membership in his community, even in his death. In fact, he visualized that his passing would be a communal event, marked by rituals whose observance would draw the members closer to each other and to him.

Yet it would not be true to say that in anticipating death, only the fear of it is to be feared. Even if the prospects of pain, invalidism, and isolation were removed, the existential issues remain: the end of being, the loss of experience, relationships, and, above all, control. The prospect of death means contemplating an unfinished story to which no more can be added. Prepared or unprepared, fearful or hopeful, everyone has sooner or later to cope with this fact. Yet, although the fact itself is predictable, the styles of coping with it are as diverse as human nature itself.

A young woman facing the probability that her illness was a terminal one put into memorable words her experience of the existential fear:

> Don't hover over my head
> you crowd me with
> your black cape

Skilled by scorned
   indifference
you parasite your
   victims
you tease
   senses with
      fearing unknowns

Why do you knowingly
   tickle
     my skin
with your
   vibrations

In night's
   darkness you
     probe to blacken
blocking
   my way—I can't
   pass you by
we play tag
   you nag me
     with your chase
running
   around in
     circles to find
      home base[2]

Not all who must face death are so articulate, so well able to express the meaning of the event for themselves and their loved ones. It is fortunate that in recent years, largely through the pioneering efforts of Elisabeth Kübler-Ross, we have begun once more to recognize the humanity of all who must die—which means all the living. The process of dying is, indeed, a living concern. As with other living concerns, we need to begin to deal with death, in one way or another, long before the event becomes imminent. Painful as the process may be, those who can contemplate death before the fact may be spared the discovery—when it is too late to do much about it—that they have not truly lived.

Anticipation of Death

We can learn much about dealing with death from the older generation. Despite the cultural taboo, many old people are quite forthright in their anticipation of death, at least with their peers. In a gathering of people in their seventies or older, one is quite likely to hear talk of funerals, past or current. The conversation is usually matter-of-fact, sometimes even a bit gleeful. It may strike younger listeners as callous or ghoulish but it is only the sober recognition that the numbers of one's peers are dwindling and that one's own turn cannot be far off—but it hasn't come yet.

The recognition may be anguished or philosophical, but is most often very concrete and simple. A woman who was preparing to enter a retirement home with minimal cooking facilities told the social worker who had been helping her to plan the move: "I won't be cooking for six anymore. This is the soup kettle I've used since my sons were babies. It's still perfectly good—but I know my daughter-in-law in Cleveland wouldn't want to send for it. She has plenty of pots and pans. Won't you take it? You have a family, and I'd like to think it was still being used." She went on to explain the care and maintenance of the enameled kettle, pointed out it was marked on the inside to measure cups and pints, and mentioned some of the highlights of its forty years of service. The gift was accepted, and with it a piece of someone's life experience.

Other ways of taking stock of one's life and preparing a legacy include making wills, patching up old quarrels, fulfilling an old dream, and deciding which pieces of unfinished business have priority. Mrs. Farnsworth, whom we met in Chapter 2, was told by her doctor that her heart had deteriorated somewhat and that if she were fifteen years younger, he would send her to a surgeon. "I couldn't be less interested," said the seventy-eight-year-old. "Suppose he could make my heart work a little better. He couldn't fix my aching joints, could he—or my eyes—or make me get less tired when I stay up late? No. My heart should do all right for another year or two. That will be long enough to finish my book." She might almost have been saying, "This coat will last another season if we turn the lining. No sense buying a new one."

Often the old make detailed and specific funeral arrangements, and seem to derive as much satisfaction from this aspect of "putting the house in order" as they once did from finishing the spring cleaning, the yard work, or the bookkeeping.

The children or younger relatives of the aged may not be nearly so ready to consider the prospect of separation. A parent who wants to talk about wills or funeral arrangements is likely to get the response "Mother, don't talk like that." Children may fear that Mother is getting morbid or depressed or senile, and try to cheer her up or distract her. Worse yet, they may feel that some lapse or negligence on their part has caused her preoccupation. If they try to cure her by extra attention and do not succeed, they are likely to feel even more guilty, as well as resentful that their efforts are unappreciated. And then, seeing their agitation, Mother may stop trying to talk about it. Such a misperception cuts off both generations from real communication and the comfort that each could be to the other.

A beloved aunt called to wish her niece a Happy New Year. The niece, keenly aware of the progressive illness from which her aunt was suffering uncomplainingly, blurted out, "That depends on you." "You fool," the aunt replied, "when my time comes it comes . . . I'm not doing anything to make it happen!" But she sounded pleased that the subject had come up. The exchange eased for both of them the weight of the awareness that each had carried alone. In this as in other matters, secrets that can be shared are not so heavy.

Time perception has a great deal to do with the way we manage our lives. "Work expands to fit the time available," according to the Peter Principle.[3] When not much time is available, we have to set priorities to accomplish the things that are really important. This is true for people of all ages, but it is particularly true for the old who cannot escape the knowledge that time, however much of it may be left to them, is not unlimited. Awareness of the limits forces one to ask, "What have I done with my life? What can I still do?"

People deal with the shortness of time in a variety of ways. Some withdraw, feeling that no new investment is worth the pain of losing it. Others intensify their involvements, or make changes allowing for new ones.

One lady in her late seventies stepped down from a volunteer editing job—her third or fourth post-retirement career—with the explanation "Life is short, and there are important things left for me to do. In the past six months, I have been made even more aware of this as the doctor bills mounted." She went on to summarize the value of the experience. "Interviewing people sometimes almost unknown to me has been like opening doors, hitherto locked, and finding a whole world inside. These people have become my friends." Yet she felt the need to free herself for the next experience.

The age at which a person accepts and begins to deal

with the fact that time is limited may be the day he perceives himself as "old." Paradoxically, that perception may keep him from ever becoming too old to grow—even on the last day of his life.

Legacies and Balance Sheets

Those contemplating the shortness of time often draw up a sort of balance sheet of the accomplishments and failures, satisfactions and disappointments of a lifetime. Was it worthwhile or not? The answer, for the individual, often lies not so much in the accomplishments of the past as in the relationships of the present.

A woman in her eighties, facing a terminal illness, reviewed the wide range of her experiences: memories of childhood, both heartwarming and frightening; immigration to a new land; marriage, separation, and reconciliation; the pride and disappointments of child-rearing; making and losing money. The great unresolved loss in her life had been the death, at twenty-one, of her younger son. Even forty years later, this memory cast a shadow over all the others. However, in the last few months of her life she developed a close relationship with her grandson, the nephew and namesake of the son who had died. They had always been fond of one another, but during this time they were able to share many thoughts and feelings that they had not spoken of before. The young man told her not only about his career and ambitions but also about the development of his personal philosophy. Grandmother was gratified to find so many of the values she had tried to convey to her children being cherished—or rediscovered—by their children. Her perception of her life began to shift. Despite grief and hardship, it had, after all, been worthwhile.

It is not only those who prepare the legacy who are

strengthened by such an exchange, but also those who receive it. If the opportunity is lost, both will be the poorer. Sometimes the opportunity is not recognized in time. After the death of a man whose relationship with his children had always appeared demanding and critical, his eldest daughter began hearing from other relatives: "He was terribly proud of you—he always hoped you would become a writer. He wanted to be one himself, you know." She was astonished, for he had never said any such thing to her. She began wondering what her father had been like as a young man, what his ambitions for himself and his children had been. His sisters might have been able to tell her, but they, too, were gone. She felt cheated of a piece of her history.

Despite a reticence about sharing feelings that may have been lifelong, it is possible to learn to share them, even in old age. Joseph Mandel learned to talk with his children after he was sixty-five. There had always been a warm bond between them, but not much explicit communication, as we have seen on page 162. As Mr. Mandel discovered that other people, including his children, were really interested in what he had to say, he was able to tell them not only about his current wishes and needs but also about his pride in his children. He had spent his working life as a shipping clerk, and was amazed that he and his wife had produced five "brilliant," highly educated children. Conveying his feelings to his sons and daughters also freed them to express their pride in him, and gave both generations a sense of continuity and accomplishment.

Preparation Without Warning

Illness or other changes may give warning that time is short. Even when there have been no external signs, however, some people seem to sense the nearness of the end and to prepare themselves accordingly. They find ways both of seeking security and of saying goodbye.

Manya Wall, a seventy-five-year-old without family or close friends, had been a regular but casual user of a senior citizens' center. She usually stopped in late in the afternoon, had a cup of coffee, and chatted for a few minutes with whoever happened to be there. One morning, however, she came in at ten o'clock, sought out a staff member she liked, and talked for nearly an hour. Even then she did not leave, but engaged in several other conversations. Early in the afternoon she complained of feeling ill. She lay down on a nearby couch and quickly sank into a coma. The staff called an ambulance and rushed her to the hospital, where it was learned that she had suffered a stroke. She never regained consciousness, and died within a few hours. Although distressed by her death, those who knew her were glad that she had somehow been able to surround herself with people who cared about her, and had not had to die alone.

Dealing with Terminal Illness

Those who have made some preparation are more likely to withstand the shock when the time comes for facing death, either for oneself or for a loved one. Yet, like all other real experiences, this one cannot be programmed in advance. We cannot know, before the fact, exactly what our reactions will be. Of all human diversity, reactions to the imminence of death are perhaps most diverse of all. Although the handling of this crisis is likely to be consistent with one's previous management of life, there may be surprises. One may experience fear and rage of unimagined intensity—or discover unsuspected capacities for serenity and endurance. Or both. But the process, more than any other experience, may result in a keener awareness of the self and the special meaning of one's life.

Stages in the Coping Process

Elisabeth Kübler-Ross has identified various stages people go through in dealing with death: denial, anger, bargaining, depression or mourning, and acceptance.[4] These are, however, only rough guidelines, and the most valuable information they provide is that dying is a process, and so is coping with it.

There are no easy answers either for those who must face the "needle's eye" of impending death or for those who must watch and endure the loss. In a society that is often death-denying, expressions of anger and grief are difficult both for the dying and for the bereaved. The needs of both are real but not always synchronized.

Families may be astonished to discover that rage is a large component of their distress. It may be directed not only at the situation that threatens to deprive them of a loved and needed person, but at the person himself. A wife, reacting to her husband's second heart attack, expressed this succinctly: "If that bastard dies, I'll kill him!" Another kind of anger may be felt by those who must watch progressive and irreversible deterioration. A son whose mother no longer recognized him gave vent to his frustration and impatience: "I wish the inevitable would happen already." Such feelings of anger are likely to result in guilt; it seems monstrous to be angry with one who is mortally ill. Family and friends may need help in dealing with such feelings before they can talk to the ill one about death and its meaning. If they cannot do so, they remain cut off from communication with each other about the very issue that is of supreme importance. The pain of impending loss is bad enough, without adding isolation to it. Painful as it may be, sharing the anger and the tears can ease bottled-up feelings and make the relationship more gratifying for all of them.

Achieving such a resolution is complicated by the fact that, for the dying person, the anticipation of death, even if consciously denied, brings its own grief. Not only the fear of the unknown but the snatching away of all that might have been creates intense frustration. Raging against the injustice of his fate, the one facing death may see his loved ones' distress as petty by comparison. As one forthright victim said to his weeping family, "What are you all crying about? It's me that's dying!"[5]

Fortunately, feelings are complex and change from day to day as well as over time. There are bound to be some periods when both the dying and the bereaved find themselves on the same wavelength. Such times may be brief, but are worth waiting for and cherishing.

Masks and Disguises

The feelings involved in facing death may not be easily identified. Fear may wear a mask of arrogance, and a desperate effort to survive may appear as irrational or disoriented behavior. (If the person is old enough, it may be called senility.)

When Mr. Barry suffered a severe heart attack at fifty-eight, he was clinically "dead" for several minutes. He was revived, but although the doctors thought he might live for several weeks or months, they held out little hope for recovery.

Mr. Barry's reactions were bewildering to his family. He was impatient to go home, but kept finding excuses not to leave the hospital. In defiance of doctors' orders, he kept removing his oxygen mask, insisting, even while his breathing grew rough and labored, that he could manage without it, and could walk right out of the intensive care unit if he chose. Yet he objected violently if his wife left the room. When the minister, an old friend, came to visit, Mr. Barry, a deacon of his church, ordered him out of the room with most unbecoming language and gestures. His wife and daughter were terribly embarrassed. They thought he must be either brain-damaged or possessed of the devil. (Mr. Barry's older sister held to the latter interpretation.)

The minister was less perturbed. He had seen fear before, and tried to help the family understand what Mr. Barry was dealing with, and why, despite his bravado, he could not tolerate being alone. There is not much that one can offer a person caught up in elemental panic, except the equally elemental reassurance of someone's presence. When they realized what was happening, Mr. Barry's family did their best to spend as much time with him as they could, and to ride out the seemingly irrational mood swings. They, too, needed reassurance and comfort, since they were trying to deal with his distress and their own simultaneously. Once aware of his need for their presence, they felt guilty about the fact that it was not possible to be with him every waking moment and still attend to the business, the household, the needs of the daughter's children, and all the myriad activities that must go on despite the approach of death.

Sources of Help

The Barrys were fortunate to have in their minister a sympathetic friend who did not panic or withdraw. Many clergymen, though by no means all, have similar skills. The physician in charge, if he is skilled in dealing with emotional as well as medical facts, can be an immeasurable source of support. Again, not all doctors are capable of, or comfortable with, such a task. The social service department of the hospital is often an excellent resource, since its members are trained to understand feelings as well as concrete problems. Nevertheless, some of them are better at it than others. Experienced nurses, who usually have the most contact with the patient, may be of great help. Volunteers, nurses' aides, even the cleaning lady may turn out to be pillars of strength—support is where you find it. The paper qualifications do not matter as much as the person's ability to be in touch with his own feelings and responsive to other people's. And do not overlook the comfort that can be gained from, and given to, other patients and their families caught up in the same process.

To Tell or Not to Tell

Controversy still rages over the question of whether a terminally ill person should be told of his diagnosis and prospects. Although some of the conflicts probably result from the fact that often doctors, as well as laymen, have great difficulty in dealing with such material, the argument boils down to truth versus hope. One position holds that if the patient is not told the truth, he or she will not have the opportunity to complete unfinished business—practical or psychological—and set his or her affairs in order according to his or her own wishes. If, in addition, there is a sense that information is being withheld, it may undercut the patient's confidence in both the physician and the family, increase feelings of isolation and panic, and make the patient less amenable to treatment. Those who take the oppo-

site position point out that the truth may destroy all hope
and undercut the patient's will to live. They also remind
us that no one can say, with certainty, how long anybody
has to live, and that any doctor can cite examples of people
still walking around who, according to their diagnoses,
should have been dead long since.

The dispute is probably not as irreconcilable as it looks.
Most people are very skillful in tuning out whatever they
are not ready to hear, as well as sensing the significance
of that which is not being stated aloud. A teenager, with
leukemia, whose condition had been discussed extensively
both with her and with her family, confided to her mother,
"If I had cancer, I wouldn't want to be told." "Neither
would I, honey," responded the mother. They both knew,
but didn't want the knowledge shoved in their faces. Likewise, a woman of eighty, suffering from a similar disease,
told her daughter, "These treatments aren't doing any
good—they only make me sick. What does that doctor think
he's doing?" The family had been careful not to give her
the exact name of her condition, but now the daughter
questioned, "Would you like to ask him more about it?"
"No. What would he tell me?" the mother replied. "I know
I'm not getting any better."

Both the young girl and the old woman had grasped the
essentials of their situations. They were fortunate that their
families were willing to be as explicit as the patients wanted
them to be. It is more difficult for those who suspect the
truth but meet with staunch denials on the part of family
and/or medical personnel.

Mrs. Lance, a woman of sixty-eight, suffered a sudden
onset of dizziness and loss of memory. Her children rushed
her to a hospital, where tests eventually disclosed the existence of a malignant brain tumor. This was removed surgi-

cally, and the patient almost immediately regained memory and the awareness of her surroundings. She appeared to be making an excellent recovery. Still, her physicians decided to use radiation as a follow-up treatment. They felt the long-term prognosis was probably poor, so in order not to worry Mrs. Lance, they did not explain what they were doing or why. Her family, understandably, were eager to assure her that all was well. However, after a few treatments she lapsed into a deep depression, became disoriented once more, and stopped responding to her family's efforts to communicate. Some of this behavior may have been due to side effects of the treatment, but what cannot be discounted is the effect on an intelligent person, who knows what radiation is used for, of having her questions and concerns ignored or denied. If temporary disorientation was anticipated as a side effect, Mrs. Lance and her family could have been prepared for this, and would probably have found it less devastating. If she suspected she was dying, it was of no help that she also feared she was losing her mind, or that she believed everyone around her was telling lies.

Calculating the Odds: The Half-Full and the Half-Empty Glass

The statistical odds for or against recovery probably have very little to do with anybody's motivation to fight for his life—not only its duration but also its quality. One person may give up although his chances look relatively good, while another may cling to even the slimmest of chances with energy and determination. A wise physician always told his patients, "There's no such thing as a twenty-five percent chance; for you, it's either a hundred percent or zero." Whether one sees the glass as half-full or half-empty depends more on the nature of his personality than on the nature of his disease.

Those who focus entirely on their chances for survival, even in the face of a contrasting reality, may appear to be denying what is real. Perhaps it is not denial so much as concentration, or, to put it another way, selective inattention. If a student is preparing for a tough exam, it is considered commendable if, in his concentration, he shuns television and radio, refuses invitations, tells his roommates to get lost, and closets himself with his books. When the dying person, obsessed by his will to live, shuts out defeat and postpones acceptance of his approaching end, he may simply be waiting until he feels prepared, in his own way and by his own rules, to test his readiness for death. Eventually, after long and debilitating illness, the prospect of death may be welcomed as a release from loneliness and pain. With such a resolution comes a sense of peace, readiness, and a yearning to rest from the struggle which has been acknowledged as futile.

Those who resist death to the last and those who welcome it are alike in attempting to enhance the quality of their lives. When the particular circumstances, as well as the reactions to them, are so various, can there be any general guidelines as to the needs of the terminally ill?

There is one great common denominator. The terminally ill person continues being himself. He is the same person as he was before the diagnosis—not a hero, a walking corpse, or a Martian. Perhaps the most difficult thing for one in that position to deal with is the tendency of friends and loved ones to treat him in a gingerly and special way. He may want to talk about the approaching event—it is the most important thing that has ever happened to him, after all—or he may not. However he handles it, he needs to be recognized as himself, lest his own sense of who he is should dissolve.

What the dying person needs most is apt to be most difficult for his friends and loved ones to provide—not only because of the foreshadowing of loss, and their natural attempts to deny or forestall it, but because the cultural taboo against death and dying may make it very hard for them to respond naturally to one on whom the seal of change has been set. He may want to talk, cry, swear, or go dancing—or all of these in turn. His friends, having no model of expectations to work from, may find this bewildering. If, however, they can overcome their reluctance and accept him at his level, they may find it an enriching experience.

Dealing with death is so alien to most of us that we are almost in the position of those who believed the earth was flat and therefore dared not venture too close to the edge. If we can find the courage to do so, however, we may discover that even at the edge of life, there is a continuation, and that those who are close to death can continue growing and giving.

For many people it is important to round off their relationships with others, perhaps giving some up immediately, closing out others with farewell visits as energy permits, and concentrating on the few that are most important and whose meaning must be explored and expressed while yet there is time.

An old woman, knowing that her time was short, told her husband of many years, "You know, I believe in a continuing cycle of life. Isn't it nice we don't have to just walk away from each other but can say a proper goodbye?" Then, regretfully, "But I know you will feel pain. I cannot bear the thought of that for you." As in other areas of life, the burdens we must watch others carry often feel heavier than our own.

St. Francis Hospital in Evanston, Illinois, which provides a great deal of nursing care to the terminally ill, utilizes a "dying person's bill of rights" in training staff for this task. It is a good summary of the needs of those facing death.

THE DYING PERSON'S BILL OF RIGHTS

I have the right to be treated as a living human being until I die.

I have the right to maintain a sense of hopefulness however changing its focus may be.

I have the right to be cared for by those who can maintain a sense of hopefulness, however changing this might be.

I have the right to express my feelings and emotions about my approaching death in my own way.

I have the right to participate in decisions concerning my care.

I have the right to expect continuing medical and nursing attention even though "cure" goals must be changed to "comfort" goals.

I have the right not to die alone.

I have the right to be free from pain.

I have the right to have my questions answered honestly.

I have the right not to be deceived.

I have the right to have help from and for my family in accepting my death.

I have the right to die in peace and dignity.

I have the right to retain my individuality and not be judged for my decisions which may be contrary to beliefs of others.

I have the right to discuss and enlarge my religious and/or spiritual experiences, whatever these may mean to others.

I have the right to expect that the sanctity of the human body will be respected after death.

I have the right to be cared for by caring, sensitive, knowledgeable people who will attempt to understand my needs and will be able to gain some satisfaction in helping me face my death.

Quality Versus Quantity

Not only are reactions to the prospect of death very personal, but the decision as to how to use the remaining time is a highly individual affair. Optimism, even stubbornness, in the face of odds has been thoroughly documented in accounts of young people's battles against disease and dysfunction. What we tend to forget is that old people may have just as much zest for living, despite aches and pains, uncooperative bodies, and unpromising diagnoses. One such was Anna Maddington, whose heart was so bad that she had to have oxygen in the house constantly, and was liable to blackouts if she tried to defrost a refrigerator or scrub a floor. Yet, between bouts of pain, she tended her geraniums, did a little baking, and proudly displayed a whole dresser top full of pictures of grandchildren. Despite her illness, she exuded an intense vitality. Sometimes, when the seizures of pain were longer and more frequent than usual, her anxious family tried to get her to consider a nursing home. "And would that keep me from dying?" Anna would ask. Her children and her doctor had to admit that it would not. "Well, then," said Anna, "what's the point?"

"Mother, we may come in here and find you dead someday!" protested her oldest daughter.

"So you may," retorted Anna stoutly. Then, at the sight of their stricken faces, her own softened. More gently, she tried again to explain. "Remember, the person least anxious to die is myself. I have the most to lose. But I don't want to live each day I have left as if I'm already dead."

Heartened by her determination as well as by her frank delight in life, the family agreed to let her do it her way. "Yes, she's very sick," they assured each other, "but not in the head." As predicted, one day Anna had a heart seizure from which she did not recover. The children had some misgivings as to whether they had done the right thing, but on the whole they were glad that they had let death find her among her geraniums and pictures, rather than in an unfamiliar and sterile environment, among strangers. "Maybe, if you let people do what they want to do—when they die—it's a lot easier for everybody," mused her daughter.

The Right to Refuse Treatment

Letting people do what they want to do becomes increasingly more difficult and complex in a time when medical science can prolong life (or a semblance of it) for longer than was possible even a few years ago, although it is often at the cost of having to endure pain, invalidism, and helplessness. Yet to refuse such treatment is usually considered medical heresy by doctors and hospital personnel and by the patients and their families. It is important for patients to know what they can anticipate, not only if they refuse recommended treatment but also if they accept it. Most people have not had much practice in asking hard questions at a time of maximum anxiety, and need a lot of help in understanding their alternatives. Some medical settings are very good at providing such help, but others seem to have the attitude that the patient has no right to pursue any course of action that might result in shortening his life, and that the less he knows about the possibilities, the better. Patients who are coping with grave illness, as well as their families, cannot be reminded too often that they have the right to ask questions and get answers, the right to a second opinion, and the right to say no.

For instance, a woman who had had one leg amputated developed a similar condition in the other. She said she would not consent to another amputation. The doctors told her that if she did not, they would wait until she was unconscious and get her husband to sign the papers. This left the patient feeling even more helpless and furious, and placed a heavy burden of guilt on the husband. If he refused, he would feel responsible for his wife's death, and if he consented, he would bring down her wrath on his head. Besides, in their entire married life, neither had ever defied the other in important decisions; before, they had always made them together. Now not only the maintenance of her life but the quality of both life and marriage were at stake.

The Nature of Hope

Those who struggle to sustain life regardless of its quality may insist that where there is life, there is hope. Hope in some form is essential to life, yet its maintenance requires a great deal of energy. When a treatment gives promising results for a while, then loses its effectiveness, it is painful to risk hoping again. For many who have been through repeated disappointments, the certainty of disaster may become easier to bear than the possibility of reprieve. It is those inside the experience who must determine how much hope they can endure. Those outside—friends, medical practitioners, even family—can only accept the decision. As suffering increases, the focus of hope may change from cure to release.

Isaac Kerschler had contended against a myriad of illnesses for many years. Emphysema made breathing a constant struggle; circulatory difficulties caused intense pain in his legs. At eighty he felt that he had had enough; he was ready to say his goodbyes. Those around him were not so ready. They urged him to get further treatments, to seek nursing-home care, or at least to accept some additional help at home. Mr. Kerschler, however, did not want to postpone his death at the cost of prolonging his suffering. Neither did he want to lose the measure of independence he still felt that he had. He insisted on staying home alone, assuring those who worried about him that he'd "manage somehow." As his family feared, and as he perhaps hoped, within a few days he was dead. Seeing his face relaxed and peaceful, freed of the torture he had endured so long, his loved ones were finally ready to view this as his last loving message to them, and to be grateful for what he had chosen to spare himself and them.

Heroic Measures and Living Wills

Isaac Kerschler's choice reflects the existence of a new problem. Not only can some conditions now be treated that would have been quickly fatal before, but "heroic measures" can often keep a heart pumping and the breath moving in and out long after all hope of recovery is past. Injections, transfusions, intravenous feedings, dialysis, breathing machines—all manner of sophisticated equipment may be brought into play. The patient may be comatose, he may have suffered irreversible brain damage; yet the efforts continue. The methods are often uncomfortable, and certainly expensive. Why this exercise in futility?

When a son, watching his dying father being artificially fed, asked the doctor why this was still necessary, the doctor's response was "The hospital cannot risk being accused of having allowed a patient to starve to death."

There are other reasons, all of which may play a part: the fascination, and trust, in the wonders of technology; the hope for a breakthrough, or a miracle; the physician's unwillingness to accept defeat; the family's sense of guilt unless "everything possible was done"; the hospital's fear of legal liability if life supports, once provided, are withdrawn. Certainly the decisions involved are not easy. Made in love and anguish and uncertainty, they are agonized over both before and after the fact. Omniscience is not within the grasp of mortals, and its lack is one of the things for which we have to learn to forgive both ourselves and others.

One of the characters in Peter De Vries's novel *The Blood of the Lamb* refers to medicine as "the art of prolonging disease." Asked why anyone would want to do that, he replies, "In order to postpone grief."[6] Perhaps the taboo against acknowledging death has produced this juggernaut in which neither the patient nor his family seems to have much to say about the quality of his survival. However that may be, the present generations must now contend with a nightmare that did not worry their forebears. Rather than only fearing premature death, before their potential is fulfilled, they must now worry about outliving their potential altogether, and having willy-nilly to endure a vegetable existence. They dread becoming a burden to themselves and everyone else, able to experience little but pain, restriction, and helplessness. We have said that age is denigrated partly because of its association with death; it is curious that one of the chief burdens of old age may be the fear of *not* being able to die!

Because of this fear, increasing numbers of people are writing "living wills," with instructions that they do not want heroic measures resorted to. The extent to which these are legally binding is questionable, but their use indicates both a concern and an attempt at solution. Rather than relying on such a document alone, it would probably be more effective to discuss one's wishes with the family or friends most likely to be available, preferably before a physical crisis supervenes. Sometimes even the concerted efforts of family and physician cannot avert or terminate futile heroics intended to prolong the spark of life; however, making a plan does provide a measure of control, and such an approach may in time modify legal interpretations as well.

The Right to Die

Some would take the issue a step further and claim the right not only to avoid extraordinary efforts to maintain life but the right to hasten death themselves if nature proves dilatory. This position has been more controversial than the opposition to heroic measures. Its opponents fear that allowing a person to choose the time of his death would open the way for others to do it for him, and would result in many deaths brought about to serve private convenience or public policy rather than individual choice. The terminally ill might be subject to pressures from family or others who find them a burden and would just as soon have them "choose" to die. Its proponents say that the death of a private citizen does no injury to society, therefore should not be a crime; and that safeguards against its abuse could be built in. The idea has no official legal sanction at present, but the "accidental" death of a person suffering from an incurable and painful disease is often treated sympathetically, with minimal investigation. Even a "mercy killing" under such circumstances is sometimes treated as gently as the law can be construed to allow. There is obviously concern about how much suffering must be required of the terminally ill.

Comfort Versus Cure

The hastening of death is not the only solution being sought for the problem of protracted suffering. Some doctors are seeking the legalization of powerful pain-killing drugs, which are not now available for medical use.[7] In addition, the hospice concept of care for the terminally ill is beginning to be tried in this country.[8] The word "hospice" originally referred to the medieval inns which were maintained for the comfort and refreshment of weary travelers. As used today in England and some other countries, it means a center for the care of those who can no longer benefit from hospital treatment. Rather than continuing futile attempts at cure, it seeks to maintain comfort and dignity. Its patients are kept as pain-free as possible and allowed to participate in whatever activities appeal to them. It is noteworthy that hospice patients—although allowed more pain-killers than is the practice in most hospitals—are described as appearing more alert and less sedated, as well as more cheerful and less depressed, than patients with similar conditions who are being cared for in traditional hospital settings.

Twentieth-century medical advances have added some new dimensions to the age-old question of how to confront death. Yet the question itself remains. The answers, garnered by centuries of human experience, have not changed very much either. The way to prepare for the end of life is to live it as fully as possible. In the words of George Papashvily, drinking a farewell toast to a dear friend, ". . . in the midst of death still we are in a life. Amen."[9]

9

Death in the Family

The Needs of Families

Those who are close to the dying have their own needs and may need help in meeting them. Having to provide support while anticipating loss, dealing with bewildering or disappointing behavior in their loved ones, encountering unacceptable feelings of weariness, impatience, or anger in themselves—the families of the dying have a heavy task. They, too, need sustenance and should not hesitate to seek it. Some of the likely sources of help were noted earlier.

Many of the needs of families—for honest information, for participation in decision-making, for a focus of hope— are the same as those of the dying patient. Some are likely to be different. For instance, the patient may project his anger and helplessness onto his family, or he may need to withdraw and disengage at a time when they yearn to strengthen the ties. This can be very hard for the family to accept when they have a keen sense of impending loss. The ups and downs of the illness, its alternating hope and discouragement, may be even more difficult for the family than for the patient whose depleted energy may provide some insulation. As one wife commented after having seen her husband through several remissions and relapses, "Everything is scarier the second time you do it."

A necessity for those close to the dying is to continue with their own lives—other relationships, work, even fun. This may seem monstrous but it is essential. No one can completely submerge himself in another's being, even when that person is supremely important and soon to be lost.

Doris Lund, mother of a teenager contending against leukemia, discovered this when her energy and patience suddenly gave out. A brief vacation, coupled with a new kind of work, helped to replenish her. "Lose Eric I might," she reflected, "[but] to lose myself along the way would be a senseless waste."[1] Such "selfishness" is essential to the survival of those close to the dying and it also helps to improve the relationship. Even when dying—especially then—nobody wants to be smothered.

Having maintained a separate identity will stand the family in good stead when death does arrive and the need for maintaining a supportive relationship gives way to the requirements of mourning.

The Necessity of Mourning

After a loss, it is necessary to mourn.

Since our culture is reluctant to acknowledge death in the first place, it is not surprising that the need for mourning is a fact often overlooked or denied. Mourning is apt to be looked upon as weakness or self-indulgence. Those who preserve a stoic calm at a funeral are commended for "taking it so well"; those who weep feel constrained to apologize for "breaking down." This lays a heavy burden of unrealistic expectations on the bereaved. Not only must they cope with the loss itself, but also with the assumption that they should be able to act as if it had not occurred. This is about as reasonable as expecting someone who has broken a leg to walk around as if nothing had happened. Those who have lost a beloved person have also sustained an injury and require a healing process. Grief is part of that process.

The Importance of Ceremonies

The first stage of grief is usually a kind of numbness of disbelief, followed by emotional pain as the reality of the loss sinks in. During this time, the bereaved must have opportunities to talk about the death, to cry, to review the life of the lost person, and, in general, to have the support and presence of those who care about them. These needs can be met, in part, through the ceremonies usually surrounding death—wake, funeral, memorial service, *shiva,* or whatever is familiar and customary to the people involved. These ceremonies provide structure during a time of transition.

It has become fashionable to brand funeral practices as archaic, uncivilized, and exploitative. Although some of the charges of exploitation may be well founded, the familiar custom does provide a shelter and a sense of continuity to those passing through emotional chaos, as well as a means of drawing together those who can share the grief and so provide support and comfort.

The ceremonies may, of course, mean more if the person who died had a share in planning for them. Carrying out his wishes then becomes another way in which the family can maintain its sense of continuity.

The Facilitation of Mourning: What Friends Can Do

Friends and acquaintances often become mute and panicky in the presence of grief, especially if they have not experienced bereavement themselves. The grieving person's experience may appear so overwhelming that friends wishing to give of themselves may feel helpless, even presumptuous. It may help to remember that their presence matters more than their words. It is not necessary to be profound. "I am so sorry" may be quite sufficient to convey one's recognition of another's pain. What does not help is any attempt to rationalize the disaster. A comment such as "It's a blessing that she didn't suffer" is an affront, not a comfort. It conveys the message that the speaker is standing outside the experience, dissociating himself from it and thereby denigrating it. When the bereaved is ready to find compensations, he will do it himself, in his own way. To attempt to do it for him only makes the work of grief more difficult, and lays upon the griever an additional burden of loneliness. If those who are with him cannot acknowledge his distress, he is isolated indeed. Furthermore, well-meant but premature efforts at "comfort" may impose an obligation to feel "comforted" on someone who, in fact, feels devastated. This is no help at all. Far from assuaging grief, it only precipitates depression and fury.

Words are not the only way of offering sympathy. Gifts of food, flowers (especially the hand-picked variety), and practical services such as transportation or baby-sitting also convey to the bereaved that they are not alone. Comfort cannot be bestowed . . . but it can grow in a nurturing environment.

The Service Provided by the Bereaved to Their Would-Be Comforters

It is generally supposed that those who visit the bereaved are providing a service, and that the mourners are the recipients. This is only a half-truth. The grief of one facilitates the mourning (perhaps of unrelated losses) of all the others. The service, therefore, is mutual.

Three students went to pay a condolence call on a friend whose sister, a girl in her twenties, had died after a long illness. They had debated whether to go at all ("Will we be intruding?" "What will we say?") but finally decided to go together for mutual support. Walking toward the house, each was inwardly shaking. Once inside, however, their tension began to subside in the flow of conversation. Their friend had been looking through her sister's sketchbook, and shared it with them. As they turned the pages, they sometimes found themselves chuckling over a particularly telling caricature. The reality of loss was sharpened— there would be no more drawings done in just that style, from that wry viewpoint. Yet the reality of the person was also underscored, as well as the warmth of the still-continuing friendships among those who had gathered to honor her memory.

When the students left, they walked slowly through the summer twilight, each immersed in her own thoughts. One remembered a visit to her grandparents' graves in a tiny cemetery in northern Wisconsin and the strange sensation of seeing her own family name on the tombstones. Another thought of her father's funeral, which she had not attended because "children should not be exposed to such things." She and a cousin had spent the time playing, boisterously, while they waited for the grownups to return from their mysterious errand. The neighbor who stayed with them had been quite annoyed—something the children could not understand at all.

After a long silence, the third student summed up the feelings of all of them by commenting, "You know, I didn't think I would be, but I'm glad we went."

A death in one's circle of friends can have effects similar to those of a snowstorm or other natural disaster. Everything stops, and people begin to take notice of each other—and of themselves.

To be present and to be sensitive to the need for presence may be more important than doing or saying anything. The new widow may need a companion as she sorts through pictures, clothing, and other mementos—someone with whom to share the memories they evoke. On the other hand, she may need to be alone for this task or may not be ready to do it at all for some time. It is important for the bereaved and those around them to be clear and to feel free to express what they really want, rather than going along with what somebody thinks they should want.

When Mr. Blair died, his older daughter and her husband came to be with Mrs. Blair for a period of time after the funeral. Feeling that her mother was immobilized by shock, the daughter took over the task of disposing of her father's possessions. She meant to be helpful, but her well-intentioned efforts defrauded Mrs. Blair of the chance to sort out her own memories in her own way and time. In the same way, children or other relatives may be in great haste to make alternative living arrangements for a surviving spouse. They want to keep Mother (or Father) from feeling lonely, when, in fact, the parent needs to feel the loneliness in order to deal with it. She (or he) needs to have family or other supports available, but not to have their grieving taken over for them.

The Task of Mourning

The healing process, after a major loss, takes a long time and cannot be hurried. In mourning, the emotional task is to incorporate the loss, to live with it and around it, to survive and to grow. This is sometimes described as learning to give up the relationship with the lost person and to find one's satisfactions elsewhere, but that is only a partial truth. Although the separation must be consummated, the value of the remembered life continues to enhance the lives of the survivors. In time, not only the encounter itself but even the experience of termination may be perceived as enriching. One does not forget, but remembers with a smile. Such tranquility, however, is the end of the process, not the beginning. At first, the loss must be experienced on all its many levels and with all its many contradictions.

Grief Has Many Faces

We usually think of grief as expressed in tears or through other outward signs of sorrow. It may be harder to recognize when it takes the form of anger, irritability, frenetic activity, profound fatigue, or physical symptoms. Yet all of these, as well as others, may be expressions of grief and stages in the mourning process.

Anger is a part of grief that is often difficult to recognize or accept. "Speak no evil of the departed" is not only a common saying but a profound feeling. Even if one heartily disliked the deceased, there is a reluctance to criticize those who can no longer defend themselves. How much more does one shrink from critical words or thoughts about the beloved! Yet even those we love most dearly are sometimes disappointing in their behavior, and their death does not change that fact. In addition to such memories, there is a more basic cause for anger—the fact of death itself. Our loved ones have gone away when we wanted them to stay, have abandoned us when we needed them. The automatic response to such frustration is anger. Since we know, rationally, that they had no choice in the matter, we push the idea away, but the feelings remain. Most of us have some difficulty accepting our feelings of anger toward those we love even when they are alive. If they die, the difficulty becomes all the greater.

Anger is more likely to be focused on the doctors or the hospital or to be directed toward ourselves, not the person who has deserted us. "If only I had made Jeff see a doctor sooner . . . or a different doctor . . . if we hadn't taken that trip . . ." And so on. Blame and self-blame are typical early grief reactions, and much of this needs to be borne alone. As a wise observer of a new widow's reaction stated, "What she really needs is her husband to tell him how angry she is with him for having left her."

Irritability

The anger of grief may also be expressed more indirectly, in a general irritability and impatience. Activities which held one's attention before may now seem to be a meaningless waste of time. The demands, and even the contributions, of others may feel like an intolerable encroachment. It is as if the bereaved were saying: "Why are these here when she is not?" It is unfortunate that, during this stage, the grieving one may alienate himself from the relationships he still has. Friends who feel put off by his apparent lack of receptivity may eventually withdraw, leaving him even more isolated. It helps if the friends can recognize the source of his behavior and let him know that they will still be available when he feels ready. Such an act of friendship is much more difficult than sympathizing with open tears, but those who can do it are friends indeed.

Frenetic Activity

Rather than withdrawing, the bereaved may fling himself into a round of constant activity. The new widower may stay late at the office, begin a long-postponed project, and take on the Boy Scouts. A recent widow, who had not worked outside the home before, approached the local volunteer office asking for "something *hard* to do." They sent her to assist teachers of mentally retarded children in the public school. This task, begun as an anodyne for pain, became a career, one that filled the emptiness of her life, and reaffirmed for her the ability still to give to others and be productive and creative despite her loss.

Not many years ago, a television program portrayed a widow who had gotten involved in exhibition dancing and won a prize as "queen of the stardust ballroom." Observers would be mistaken to suppose that these busy, "happy" folk experience no grief. Activity can be a means of survival, a way of distancing oneself from the loss until the strength to deal with it has been gained. It can also become a permanent and desperate effort to escape from facing pain. In that case, the reluctant mourner finds that he has to run faster and faster to stay where he is, and that the anodynes have become addictive without providing comfort. For such people, the greatest kindness friends and family can perform is to facilitate, perhaps even force, expressions of grief—to encourage talking about the deceased, reminiscing about the past, themselves giving vent to anger and tears—and thus help to ease the emotional constipation that so often results from prolonged denial of feelings.

Fatigue

Unusual fatigue may be experienced not only by those who have greatly increased their level of activity but also by those who continue their daily rounds much as they always have. They can't seem to get enough sleep, morning always comes too early, and their energy does not last through the day. Sometimes this is experienced not so much as weariness but as a lack of zest and enthusiasm, even for activities previously enjoyed. This may be puzzling to the bereaved as well as to their friends, since they see no reason to be so tired. What they forget is that bereavement, like any other trauma, is exhausting, and that the process of recovery requires energy and time.

In addition to fatigue, there may be other physical symptoms, which can range from a general feeling of malaise to mimicry of the illness of the person who has died. Perhaps this is similar to the "phantom limb pains" felt by an amputee. Although such a degree of physical identification is extreme, lesser symptoms can be quite common. The survivor may tire more quickly, catch cold more easily, or take longer to recover from any illness he may contract. On the other hand, there can also be a lessening of physical symptoms once the need to offer support and care to the dying person has passed. The point is that bereavement, anticipated and actual, is a physical as well as an emotional stress. The bereaved need to be gentle with themselves and pay as much attention to their need for rest and proper diet and avoidance of stress as do any other convalescents.

This does not mean, of course, that mourners should avoid all activity. Far from it. However, the kind and amount of activity that are helpful are highly individual matters. Some fling themselves into work or social life or volunteer service and can hardly bear to be alone or unoccupied. Others need a period of solitude and withdrawal before they can begin to move toward reinvolvement with life.

While all the many faces of grief can be present in the early stages of bereavement, in time they begin to dissipate and eventually pass.

When they do not pass in a reasonable amount of time, or if self-blame persists, grief can degenerate into guilt and depression. While it is easy to assume that guilt and depression go hand in hand, we must be careful to differentiate the two states. Regardless of the way in which mourning manifests itself, whether it be through anger, lack of energy, irritability, or frenzied attempts to run away from one's thoughts, grief is a process, one that moves toward new equilibrium.

It may take a long time before the nature of that equilibrium begins to appear. However, if months, or even years, after the event the bereaved is still reacting to his loss in exactly the same way, this is evidence that the process of recovery has gotten stuck. For instance, the one who has suffered a loss may never talk about it, or he may talk incessantly—but always in the same way, almost in the same words. The lack of change is a clue that the dynamic process of grief has been replaced by the static condition of depression. If that happens, the sufferer may need more than the help of friends in order to continue with his recovery. Professional help is available and can do much to alleviate misery and stimulate optimism and growth.

Each Lost Relationship Has Its Own Grief

No two relationships are exactly alike, and the grief at the severing of each will also be unique. The death of one friend affects us differently from the death of another. The loss of a sister is not the same as the loss of a parent, spouse, or child. The death of a child may be particularly devastating, because it feels so unnatural and unjust. Spouses know that one must survive the other, and most people expect to survive their parents. These losses, however painful, are inevitable. To survive one's child, however, is not the way the life cycle is supposed to be arranged. Parents who lose a child may feel not only bereft but singled out, laden with a special burden that no one else has to bear. Their distress is likely to be complicated by guilt—the feeling (irrational though it may be) that they must have failed in the caretaking role. This is generally understood when the child is an infant, an adolescent, or a young adult. However, the relationship and the sense of responsibility prevail regardless of the age of child or parents. The loss of a son who succumbs to a heart attack at forty—or sixty—is no less an outrage to his parents than if he had been twenty—or two.

Although the death of a child is assumed to be exceptional, it is not as unusual as we suppose. Of the users of a senior citizens' center, most of them in their mid-seventies or older, almost a third were known to have survived at least one of their children. It is one of the little-recognized hazards of aging that the older generation may turn out to be tougher than their sons and daughters. When that happens, the elders suffer the "survivors' guilt" and disappointed expectations of younger parents, as well as the loss of a portion of their own support system. Not only the children but the grandchildren may prove to be vulnerable. A couple in their eighties whose son had attended to their shopping needs lost this help when their grandson developed leukemia. The financial, physical, and psychic energies of the whole family were diverted to the young man's care and treatment, and the grandparents were left stranded as well as distressed. The death of a child may be felt as parental failure or loss of major support; the death of a grandchild adds to these insults the loss of one's chief guarantee of immortality.

One Loss Reactivates Others—and Assists in the Healing Process

One who is going through the loss of an important person is likely to recall all the other losses in his life. It is as if time rolled backward and the earlier experiences became as vivid as flashbacks in a movie.

An old woman whose fifty-year marriage had just been ended by her husband's death kept repeating over and over, in a sort of chant, "Where is my mother who died when I was three? Where is my sister who died in the old country?" For the moment, they were as real as they had been in her childhood, their losses as "present" as the loss of her husband two days earlier.

Sometimes a loss other than death can have the same effect. A vigorous grandmother who had prided herself on her independence had a stroke that left one arm and leg partially paralyzed. She found cleaning, shopping, and other household tasks so difficult that she eventually gave up her apartment and moved in with her daughter. For several months thereafter she talked a great deal about the death of her husband, twenty years earlier, as well as the loss of a daughter who had died at the age of eleven. Her family thought she was becoming senile, because these events were so far in the past. Actually, she was mourning the loss of her mobility and independence, was reacting to the loss of her former life—and remourning the loss of her husband and child.

Family and other observers often feel that the re-experiencing of earlier griefs, when piled on current losses, must be overwhelming. However, the reverse is likely to be true. A new grief may open another opportunity for resolving an old one, much like draining a wound incompletely healed and still festering under the scab. Attempting to distract the sufferer only results in once more interrupting the healing process. It would be far better to treat the remembered losses as real but unfinished business that needs to be dealt with. Too often, sorrow is regarded as a static condition that, once acknowledged, can never be resolved or changed; the only hope is concealment or distraction. The truth is the very opposite: only by experiencing the pain, shedding the tears, and addressing the feelings can one be freed to go on to the next stage of growth. The grief work following a death can no more be successfully avoided than the labor preceding a birth. Or rather, it can be and all too often is; but the results for the one who cannot mourn are similar to stillbirth—and aspects of his personality remain unrealized or inaccessible. For such people, later events may offer a second chance to mourn, and so to heal the old wounds along with the new.

Ending Unsatisfactory Relationships: A Paradox

It is hardest to terminate a relationship that has been unsatisfactory or conflicted.

At first glance this seems ridiculous: surely it is most difficult to give up a relationship deeply enjoyed? Surprisingly, that is not so. Losing a beloved person is painful, but it is a different kind of pain. It may be initially devastating, but it is far less likely to be accompanied by the haunting regret for what never was, the guilty sense that one must not have tried hard enough, or the frustrated anger that the response sought was never quite forthcoming. It is easier to relinquish a relationship in which something has been achieved than one which has gotten nowhere. The good relationship caresses and comforts in its lingering effect, and the bereaved soon finds that the earlier enrichment of his life has fortified him to continue to live in a fulfilling way. On the other hand, the surviving partner of an unsatisfying marriage, the child who has tried all his life to win a parent's approval, the sister whose sense of rivalry stood in the way of friendship with her brother—these are the ones who suffer most when death confirms the fruitlessness of their efforts. As John Greenleaf Whittier wrote:

> For of all sad words of tongue or pen,
> The saddest are these: "It might have been!"

The Nature of Courage

The mourner's acceptance and integration of loss are greatly affected by the quality of the life of the person whose death is mourned. John Donne's words "any man's death diminishes me" apply not only to death. Failure to live as fully as possible diminishes the observers as well as the individual. To have one's time cut short is tragic, but the ultimate tragedy is not to have used the time one had. Conversely, anyone's fullness of living replenishes those around him, because while his potential may have been unfulfilled, it was not unused.

This has been illustrated by the fact that a number of books about young people contending against eventually fatal illnesses have become best-sellers. Perhaps their attraction lies not so much in the youth of the protagonists or in the tragic odds against them as in their refusal to settle for being less than themselves. That is the essence of courage, and it is not the prerogative of any age or stage in life.

Grief Versus Guilt

Grief is essentially a healing process; it is guilt that is destructive. But guilt, like grief, can be relieved by the expression of it. Acknowledging one's sense of rebelliousness for having wished it otherwise, of feeling incomplete, of having been cheated of the chance to make things better, of somehow being responsible or having brought on the tragedy, of fearing retribution—these are the conflicts which must first be admitted to oneself, and then shared if a peaceful acceptance is to be achieved.

Annabelle was thirteen when her mother died. Her family did not cry, nor did they talk about it. Annabelle believed she had not helped her mother to stay alive—she did not do enough for her, she was not as obedient as she should have been, she had really felt closer to her father.

Ten years passed, and the young woman sought out an old family friend—a woman who had grown up with her mother and who had become a courtesy "aunt" to Annabelle and her siblings. "Tell me about my mother," she begged. "I don't remember enough." She could not ask her father, or her grandmother, or her mother's only sister.

"I don't want to remind them and hurt them," she said. And their silence indicated to her that they did not wish to share their pain with her, and her guilt deepened. She was alone and deserved to remain so.

"Aunt" Ruth began to share her own recollections with Annabelle—her memories of the giving, loving mother whose joy was in doing for and with her family. She recalled the sudden onset of the infectious disease and the frantic efforts of the doctors and hospital staff to combat it. When she finished, Annabelle's eyes were shining with tears. "Oh, I wish Daddy and Grandma Grace could have told me that," she burst out.

"Maybe they could, if you asked them," Ruth suggested.

When Annabelle went home, she plucked up her courage and asked her grandmother, who lived with Annabelle and her father, to tell her about her mother's childhood. Heartened by the warmth of Grandmother's response, she then began asking her father about how he and her mother had met—their courtship—their wedding day—the places they had lived—the births of the children. He, too, responded, awkwardly at first, then eagerly. Pictures, scrapbooks, letters long shut away in drawers were hauled out and examined and caressed. Finally, Annabelle asked about the day when mother first became ill and about the day on which she died. When the tears came, they came for all of them, and washed away the heaviness and the constriction that each had borne in private agony. Suddenly, they were no longer alone, and memories of the mother warmed them and thus brought her back into existence.

Ten years is a long time, but for some people it takes even longer before they can examine the pain and begin to resolve it. The important thing is that there be relief in addressing the memory. For another mother—a woman of seventy-seven—it was forty years after her husband's death that she was finally able to tell her daughter, who was then fifty years old, about her experience of the funeral—a sharing which tightened the emotional bond between the two still-bereaved women, and which freed the mother from the pain of the long-harbored secret.

Death as a Teacher

Perhaps the approach of death is less strange and fearful to those who have met it before.

Judy Walters's husband, Bert, had died of cancer at age thirty. The two of them had been very close during their brief married life, and they shared the experience of Bert's illness as they had shared everything else—the shock of the diagnosis, the hope and fear as treatments worked for a while and then lost their effectiveness, the growing recognition that nothing was going to help. They did not hide from each other their knowledge that Bert was dying, and so they were able to grieve together instead of separately.

After Bert's death, Judy took a job with an agency serving elderly people. One of her clients was Morris Sklar. At seventy-two, Mr. Sklar had learned that he had cancer. He decided that he wanted to move closer to his daughter, who lived in a distant part of the city. Judy would meet with the two of them to consider what the best plan would be. Sometimes the arguments were stormy. Mr. Sklar's daughter, in her anxiety, wanted him to have as much protection as possible, while he was reluctant to give up his independence a minute sooner than he had to. For a while he was able to manage in an apartment hotel. There was a dining room if he didn't feel like cooking, and on good days he could take long walks by the lake. When Judy visited, he would tell her about these excursions—the perfect shell he had found, the children building sand castles, the shore birds he had seen. "Don't usually see that kind around here," he explained. "Must be close to migration time." He broke off to apologize for "chattering." "Sue never wants to listen to this stuff," he added. "Too busy worrying about me."

When Judy talked to the daughter, she tried to remind her that her father was still enjoying his life and that she could enjoy it with him rather than only seeing herself as a caretaker. This was a new idea to Sue, but she tried to use it.

As Mr. Sklar's disease progressed, the hotel arrangement became unworkable. Reluctantly, he entered a nursing home, where Judy continued to visit him. Although he knew his illness was terminal, he did not seem fearful of death. He spent most of the visits telling Judy about his life as a young man, his later accomplishments, his family. His one regret seemed to be that he did not have a closer relationship with his daughter. "I can't talk to her like I can to you." Judy reminded him that we can be disappointed and angry with those we love, and still love them, and that his daughter's worry about him might make her sharp-tongued and inattentive. "I know, I know," he sighed.

Judy also talked to Sue about listening, about using the time they still had, rather than wasting it in vainly wishing for more. What was the use of more if these passing days were discarded?

One day when Judy came in, Mr. Sklar gave her a wry smile. "That Sue," he said. "I do believe she's getting smarter. Told me this morning she saw one of those birds I was telling you about. Didn't know what it was, but she had sense enough to ask. I told her it was a traveler." Judy smiled back.

Mr. Sklar grew steadily weaker. He welcomed Judy's visits, but often could not talk much. One day, however, he seemed unusually animated. They talked for a long time, mostly about his daughter. "She's really good," he said at last, "but she's a worrier." He gave Judy a questioning, almost pleading look. "You'll still talk to her—afterwards?" he asked. "She'll need you." "Of course," Judy reassured him. Mr. Sklar gave her another long, searching look, then closed his eyes as if satisfied. "I'm tired now, Judy," he said. "I'm going to rest—but don't go yet. Talk to me a little longer. I'll be listening."

So Judy sat beside him, stroking the thin hand. She talked quietly—not about his life's accomplishments anymore, or about his daughter; that had all been said. She told him about the wind ruffling the lake, and about the colors of the maple leaves outside the window. A tune came into her head and she hummed it, than sang the words softly. Mr. Sklar smiled a little and squeezed her fingers, but did not open his eyes again. After a while she leaned over and laid a light kiss on the wasted cheek. "Goodbye, Mr. Sklar," she whispered. She left the room and walked slowly home, feeling sad but satisfied. Mr. Sklar had resolved as much of his concerns as he could have, and had delegated the rest.

As Judy had anticipated, Mr. Sklar died that weekend. Her task with him was completed. But there was still the task of helping Sue and the many other Mr. Sklars and Sues her job had waiting for her. To each she would bring a part of herself, helped by the wisdom and experience her own tragedy had brought her. And with each new encounter, her life with Bert and her understanding of herself would take on a new and deeper dimension.

Like Judy, others who have worked through the grief of bereavement often find a new dimension of selfhood.

This is, perhaps, the meaning of "Blessed are they that mourn: for they shall be comforted." (Matthew 5:4.) It is surely true that those who cannot or will not mourn shall *not* be comforted, but are doomed to remain half alive, arrested in their growth and sense of feeling intact.

Epilogue
"Therefore Choose Life"

Why do we sometimes call the years after sixty "the growing years?" Marked by retirement, declining health, loss of spouse or friends, and other reminders of impending death, the final decades of life are more likely to be feared than welcomed. Yet these are also the years in which second careers are begun and long-cherished plans for travel and new activities realized. Grandchildren or other young people provide links to both past and future. Although one never stops being a parent to one's children, or a child to one's parents, the relationship changes over time, and may increase in mutuality as children become adults. Most of all, individuality becomes both more complete and more obvious in the later years of life. At eighty, after a lifetime of coping with all kinds of problems, having experienced triumph and disappointment, joy and sorrow, love and loss and replenishment, one is much more specifically himself or herself than one was at forty, or twenty, or ten.

The beauty of old faces is too often overlooked. It may be captured by an inspired photographer or painter, and enhance museum walls, yet may be unseen by the subjects or their associates. A young woman expressed admiration for the loveliness of an eighty-two-year-old friend, whose face with its classic bone structure might have launched the ships of Troy. "Oh," said the old woman, "you should have seen me when I was younger." She pointed to a picture of herself at twenty-five. The face was smooth and pretty, and indistinguishable from dozens of other twenty-five-year-old faces. The imprint of character developed by years of living had not yet made its appearance, and the beautiful bones were obscured by the round cheeks of youth. Yet when she looked in the mirror, this woman saw only an "old," therefore "ugly," reflection, and sighed for her former charms! Perhaps, as the aged population increases, television and Madison Avenue may learn to give us more accurate images of old people, as they have done to some extent with other minority groups. After all, the old are the one minority to which we will all belong eventually, if we live so long!

It is unfortunately true that some people never do much growing at any age. At eighty-five they may still be waiting for the magic door to open, the bluebird of happiness to arrive and make life beautiful without any effort from them. Meanwhile, they impose all kinds of unrealistic expectations on their friends and children, who should somehow atone for the bluebird's failure to appear. These expectations may increase as physical frailty sets in, and may, as a result, be blamed on the "aging process." Nevertheless, expecting someone else to do your living for you has nothing to do with age. It is just as futile at fifteen as at eighty-five. The difference lies in one's perception of how much time remains to correct the situation, and sometimes in one's needs for physical care as well.

The burden of regret for an unused life is indeed a terrible one. It is, however, a burden that only the person concerned can do much about. Sometimes the realization that time is short does precipitate action, no matter how belatedly, and can salvage one's sense of having lived a full life. The Japanese movie *To Life* describes a man confronted with a diagnosis of terminal cancer who uses his remaining time to do some of the things he has always postponed before.

Children and younger relatives worry about the older person's need for care, and may be faced with responsibilities for which they have little preparation. Yet their anxiety may be due less to the unfamiliar details of arranging for care than to their own or the older person's expectation that they "should" be able to make everything turn out beautifully. They cannot, and trying to live up to such an expectation only leads to resentment and disappointment on both sides.

Old people have widely varying needs and expectations, and so do younger ones. Most of all, people of any age need to exercise the right to be themselves. A balance may have to be struck between fulfilling one's own needs and those of other people, but to deny one's own needs altogether is always a futile waste. Such an effort is likely to be unsuccessful even in satisfying the person for whom one is "sacrificing" oneself. A story is told of an old man who was dying. He told his wife proudly, "Well, my dear, I'm thankful that I've always eaten the crusts and left you the soft bread." "Oh, John," his wife sighed, "and I love crusts so!"

Older and younger members of families may enjoy their relationships more if they remember that growth does not mean perfection. Disappointments and anger need not mean that there is nothing to cherish. One may still feel pride in one's children even if they do not visit daily, and Grandmother's recollections and pithy wisdom may be appreciated even if she is adamant about the evils of drink. Changes may occur when least expected, and all the generations may be astonished at each other's mellowing.

Changes in the meaning of a relationship also occur even after the relationship itself has been ended by death. The survivors rework what was begun during the life of the one who is gone, and may continue to gain both strength for themselves and appreciation of the life that has ended.

Growth at any age involves some degree of combat and struggle. The fact that old people are contending with their adversities does not mean that they are failing. On the contrary, it proves that they are alive and well, and living on this earth.

An example of such joyful combat is the successful, elegant couple who had lived a life of grace and culture, but who had always valued the meaning of work and accomplishment. He, eighty-two, and she, seventy-six, ruled their families with patriarchal grandeur. Over the years, they had communicated that they expected family solidarity to be perpetuated, and no one was ever absent from the celebrations the couple organized on many annual occasions. Help in the preparation offered by the younger relatives was refused; she continued to cook the family favorites and he supported her need to do so.

They had a summer home which was the center of many of these family reunions. An official opening on Memorial Day, a big cookout on the Fourth of July, and the closing festivities on Labor Day weekend were highlights around which summer vacations and family plans were made.

Each year these demands became more and more difficult for her to contemplate. She was finally prevailed upon to accept some help in the kitchen. Still she saw it as her duty to work right along with everyone else, and she was clearly in charge of all plans and their execution. She indicated he wouldn't want it any other way; he objected that she did not know how to accept help—and both continued as they always had. With one major difference: little by little, summer after summer, there would creep into their anticipation of another season the expression of doubt— could they continue for another round; would they make it to the end; how could they plan for next year, at their age? And as each summer drew closer to the end, their confidence and their sense of success increased; they ended each summer with a greater sense of triumph. They had beaten the system for another year!

Beating the system, triumphing over impossible odds, is what life is all about. "Therefore choose life."

Appendixes
Where and How to Look for Help

Knowing where to find services, both advisory and practical, is often a problem. The resources listed below can help in locating answers.

I. SOURCES OF REFERRAL

Community Referral Services

Information about available services may be provided at one location by an "umbrella" organization for all social service, health and welfare agencies in a given community. Such an organization may be called the United Way, Community Chests and Councils, Council for Community Services, Welfare Council, or some similar title. A community referral service can give information on services provided by any member agency, and can often provide information about other services available through government, civic, or commercial sources.

Telephone Directories

A. Social Service Agencies

The classified section of the local telephone directory may list helping agencies under titles such as "Social Service

Organizations," "Health and Welfare Organizations," "Senior Citizens Service Organizations," or "Community Centers." Big-city directories often have indexes which cross-reference various categories and make a particular type of agency easier to find.

B. Help at Home

In addition to service agencies, the directories list commercial providers of help at home under titles such as "Employment Agencies," "Domestic Help," "Nurses Registries," "Home Health Care," or "Meals on Wheels."

Before using any commercial provider, one should check its performance with other users, with the Better Business Bureau, and/or with state licensing agencies.

C. Equipment

Suppliers of specialized equipment for care in the home, such as wheelchairs, hospital beds, even adult diaper service, may be listed under "Hospital Equipment and Supplies," "Physical Therapy Equipment and Supplies," "Orthopedic Appliances," or the name of the item needed. Equipment can sometimes be rented as well as purchased, and Medicare may cover part of the cost if the need is certified by a physician.

If the need for equipment or services arises following hospitalization, the social service department of the hospital should be able to assist with referral to appropriate resources.

Public Libraries

A. Especially in smaller communities, the librarian is often a good source of information about what is available.

B. In addition, libraries may stock, or can obtain, directories of service-providing agencies.

C. The titles and duties of government agencies vary

from state to state, and a good reference librarian can help determine the appropriate sources.

D. Libraries are the usual providers of Braille materials, large-print books and newspapers, and talking books for the blind and the visually handicapped. They often stock audio-visual materials for the general public as well. Groups of citizens who are interested in a particular kind of material can often obtain it in this way.

E. Libraries stock or have lists of publications, pamphlets, and reports under such topics as "Aging," "Gerontology," "Geriatrics," or more general headings, such as "Health, Education and Welfare," "Mental Health," "Social Security," "Retirement," and so on. The U.S. Government Printing Office, Washington, D.C. 20402, and the U.S. Public Health Publications, National Clearing House for Mental Health Information, Washington, D.C. 20402, are important sources of such literature.

F. Public and local college and university libraries (if available) should have a number of books and periodicals that are published for the general public as well as for the academic community. A librarian can assist in locating specific information or subjects addressed in books. Periodicals published by special-interest groups such as organizations or associations, as well as government agencies, cover generalized and special subjects, and are valuable in expanding resource information. Notable among such periodicals are:

Aging, published by the Administration on Aging, Department of Health, Education and Welfare, Washington, D.C. 20201

Modern Maturity, published by the American Association of Retired Persons, Washington, D.C. 20036

Social Security Bulletins, Social Security Administration, Washington, D.C. 20201

Senior Citizens News, National Council of Senior Citizens, Washington, D.C 20005

Newspapers
A. The newspaper may be a source of help through its classified or "Help Wanted" section. One should screen individuals located in this way by getting in touch with former users to obtain references and by interviewing the individuals.

B. Many newspapers have a public information department, or one that provides a combination of advocacy and resource-finding services. This may be called "hot line," "action line," or some similar title. (Local radio stations may also have a public service program; "Call for Action" is one such program broadcast on a national network.)

Religious Organizations
In addition to individual congregations which sometimes have service networks of their own, information or services can often be located through organizations such as Catholic Charities, Lutheran Welfare, the Jewish National Fund, or the local ministerial association.

Medical Agencies
Referrals to physicians and other health specialists may be obtained through the American Medical Association, 535 North Dearborn Street, Chicago, Illinois 60610 (or its state and county affiliates), and through local hospitals. For specifics on evaluating such referrals, see Chapter 7.

Help with special health problems are frequently addressed by associations bearing the name of the disease or affliction.The American Cancer Society, the Cystic Fibrosis Association, the American Foundation for the Blind, the

American Heart Association, and so on, usually have branch offices and local addresses. Others, although of national character, have a single headquarters address. The Paget's Disease Foundation, Inc. (325 Engle Street, Tenafly, New Jersey 07670), the Committee on the Treatment of Intractable Pain (Suite 302, 2001 S Street, N.W., Washington, D.C. 20009), and others may be known to your doctor or local hospital through their publications and publicity.

Most of the national health organizations are engaged in fund-raising, research, and publication. A few, like the American Cancer Society, 219 East 42nd Street, New York, New York 10021, provide some direct service. The National Hospice Organization, 765 Prospect Street, New Haven, Connecticut 06511, will refer to existing service organizations. The National Multiple Sclerosis Society, 205 East 42nd Street, New York, New York 10017, will help locate appropriate medical resources. It is advisable to write to the national headquarters if no local office is listed in your telephone directory.

When an overall diagnosis seems indicated, there are two diagnostic centers for the elderly which accept patients from other parts of the country:

1. Philadelphia Geriatric Center, 5301 Old York Road, Philadelphia, Pennsylvania 19141

2. Johnston R. Bowman Health Center for the Elderly, Rush-Presbyterian-St. Luke's Medical Center, 710 S. Paulina Street, Chicago, Illinois 60612

Government Agencies

These may be listed as city, county, state, or federal. Some big cities, which have government agencies in all four categories, have telephone indexes which combine them according to the specific service: i.e., "Services for Senior

Citizens," "Transportation," "Consumer Complaints," "Welfare," "Medicaid," and so on.

A "Countrywide Information and Referral" resource list is published by the Administration on Aging, 330 Independence Avenue, S.W., Washington, D.C. 20201—ask for DHEW (SRS) 72-20907. Those seeking a broader overview may be interested in *Publications of the Administration on Aging*, available from the same source. This booklet lists forty-three publications on various concerns of elderly citizens, including retirement planning, consumer guides, employment opportunities, home-delivered meals, transportation, and legal matters.

II. ORGANIZATIONS OF AND FOR OLDER PEOPLE

American Association of Homes for the Aging
529 14th Street, N.W.
Washington, D.C. 20004

American Association of Retired Persons
1225 Connecticut Avenue, N.W.
Washington, D.C. 20036

American Geriatrics Society
10 Columbus Circle
New York, New York 10019

Gray Panthers
6342 Greene Street
Philadelphia, Pennsylvania 19144

Institute of Retired Professionals
New School of Social Research
60 West 12th Street
New York, New York 10014

International Senior Citizens Association, Inc.
11753 Wilshire Boulevard
Los Angeles, California 90025

National Caucus on the Black Aged, Inc.
1730 M Street, N.W.
Suite 811
Washington, D.C. 20036

National Council of Senior Citizens
1511 K Street, N.W.
Room 202
Washington, D.C. 20005

National Organization for Women (NOW),
  Task Force on Older Women
434 66th Street
Oakland, California 94609

National Retired Teachers Association
1225 Connecticut Avenue, N.W.
Washington, D.C. 20036

National Tenants Organization, Inc.
Suite 548
425 13th Street, N.W.
Washington, D.C. 20004

Oliver Wendell Holmes Association
381 Park Avenue South
New York, New York 10016

Retired Professionals Action Group
Suite 711
200 P Street, N.W.
Washington, D.C. 20010

III. SOURCES OF HELP

Social Service Agencies
These counsel families and individuals about family relationships and offer long- or short-term planning. They can often assist in locating resources for help at home or respite care. In addition to community agencies, social service departments exist in many hospitals to provide help with discharge planning and post-hospital care. Check local telephone directories (see Sources of Referral, above) or write for address of nearest local agency. Some examples of these are:

Family Service Association of America
44 East 23rd Street
New York, New York 10010

American Red Cross
17th and D Streets, N.W.
Washington, D.C. 20006

Salvation Army, National Headquarters
120 West 14th Street
New York, New York 10011

>   Eastern Headquarters
>   120 West 14th Street
>   New York, New York 10011
>
>   Central Headquarters
>   860 North Dearborn Street
>   Chicago, Illinois 60610
>
>   Southern Headquarters
>   P.O. Box 5236
>   Atlanta, Georgia 30307

Western Headquarters
P.O. Box 3846
San Francisco, California 94119

The American Lutheran Church
Division of Social Service
422 South 5th Street
Minneapolis, Minnesota 55415

Travelers Aid Association of America
44 East 23rd Street
New York, New York 10010

Home Care Agencies
These provide help with household chores and personal care, usually for a limited period. About half of the homemaker and home health aide programs in the country are certified for Medicare reimbursement.

If you cannot find one through your physician, hospital, or Visiting Nurse Association, write to one of the following for the address of the nearest local agency:

Homemakers Home and Health Care Services
3651 Van Rick Drive
Kalamazoo, Michigan 49001

National Council for Homemaker-Home Health
    Aide Services, Inc.
67 Irving Place
New York, New York 10003

Visiting Nurses, National League for Nursing
10 Columbus Circle
New York, New York 10019

Day Care

Day-care centers or day hospitals for adults are being developed in some communities as an alternative to twenty-four-hour nursing-home care. Such programs provide supervision and social stimulation for the elderly person, as well as respite for the caretaker. As the service is a new one, no national directory yet exists. To determine if one exists in your community, check with hospital or community social service departments, senior citizens' organizations, or the Administration on Aging. (See pp. 259 and 265.)

Nutrition

A. *Meals on Wheels.* Hot and/or cold meals are delivered to the homebound. Such programs are operated and funded locally, sometimes with federal participation. To find one in your community, see Sources of Referral, above.

B. *Congregate Meals.* Available at low cost in various community locations, such as churches, schools, senior citizens' centers, this program is federally funded (Title VII, Older Americans Act). The local area agencies on aging listed in the telephone directory under "Government Offices," "Senior Citizens Programs" or "Social Service Organizations—Aging," often administer the program and are good referral sources for this service.

Recreation Facilities

Recreation programs for older adults often exist in community centers serving diverse age groups, such as the Jewish Community Centers or the Y.M.C.A. and the Y.W.C.A.

In addition, there are many centers especially for older people. Directories of Senior Citizens Centers throughout the country are published by:

National Council of Senior Citizens
1511 K Street, N.W.
Washington, D.C. 20005

and

National Council on Aging
1828 L Street, N.W.
Washington, D.C. 20006

IV. GOVERNMENT PROGRAMS AND SERVICES FOR THE ELDERLY

Programs for the Elderly
A. ACTION
   806 Connecticut Avenue, N.W.
   Washington, D.C. 20525

Centralized coordinated volunteer activities for the elderly, among them:

   1. Retired Senior Volunteers Program (RSVP)

      ACTION
      806 Connecticut Avenue, N.W.
      Washington, D.C. 20525

Community activities tailored to the interests of the older volunteers.

   2. Foster Grandparents

      ACTION
      806 Connecticut Avenue, N.W.
      Washington, D.C. 20525

Volunteer work by aged persons with children on a daily one-to-one basis.

3. For information about other ACTION programs, write directly to ACTION.

B. Senior Aides
National Council of Senior Citizens
1511 K Street, N.W.
Washington, D.C. 20005

Part-time work for retired persons in public and private service programs.

C. Senior Community Service Aides Programs

National Council on Aging
1828 L Street, N.W.
Washington, D.C. 20006

Part-time employment in public programs.

Green Thumb, Inc.
1012 14th Street, N.W.
Washington, D.C. 20005

Part-time work in community improvement and beautification.

Government Agencies for the Elderly

U.S. Administration on Aging
Office of Human Development
Office of the Secretary
U.S. Department of Health, Education and Welfare
330 Independence Avenue, S.W.
Washington, D.C. 20201.

Administers housing, nutrition, and other direct service programs (see Appendix III—Sources of Help) under the

Older Americans Act. State offices may also provide information on other community services for the elderly. Since titles vary from state to state and there may also be city or county branches, write to the above address for the name and location of the nearest area agency on aging, or contact the regional office for address nearest you.

Regional Offices:

Region I (Conn., Maine, Mass., N.H., R.I., Vt.)
J. F. Kennedy Federal Bldg.
Government Center
Boston, Mass. 02203
Region II (N.J., N.Y., Puerto Rico, Virgin Islands)
26 Federal Plaza, SRS, AoA
New York, New York 10007
Region III (Del., D.C., Md., Pa., Va., W.Va.)
P.O. Box 12900
Philadelphia, Pa. 12900
Region IV (Ala., Fla., Ga., Ky., Miss., N.C., S.C., Tenn.)
50 Seventh St., N.E., Rm. 404
Atlanta, Ga. 30323
Region V (Ill., Ind., Mich., Minn., Ohio, Wis.)
433 West Van Buren, Rm. 712
New Post Office Bldg.
Chicago, Ill. 60607
Region VI (Ark., La., N. Mex., Okla., Tex.)
1114 Commerce St.
Dallas, Tex. 75202
Region VII (Iowa, Kans., Mo., Nebr.)
601 East 12th St.
Kansas City, Mo. 64106

Region VIII (Colo., Mont., N. Dak., S. Dak., Utah, Wyo.)
19th and Stout Sts., Rm. 9017
Federal Office Bldg.
Denver, Colo. 80202
Region IX (Ariz., Calif., Hawaii, Nev., Samoa, Guam, T.T.)
50 Fulton St., Rm. 406
Federal Office Bldg.
San Francisco, Calif. 94102
Region X (Alaska, Idaho, Oreg., Wash.)
1319 2nd Ave., Mezzanine Floor
Arcade Bldg.
Seattle, Wash. 98101

Social Security Administration
U.S. Department of Health, Education and Welfare
Washington, D.C. 20201.
Provides old-age, survivors, dependents, and disability benefits; also administers Medicare. Most localities have their own Social Security offices, which accept and assist with applications for benefits. If telephone directory does not have a separate listing, see "U.S. Government—Department of Health, Education and Welfare."

U.S. Department of Labor,
Manpower Administration
Washington, D.C. 20201.
Information regarding work opportunities for older adults.

Department of Public Aid. Check telephone directory for local office, usually listed under city, county, or state government "Welfare Services."

Source Notes

1 Social Changes

1. Robert N. Butler and Myrna I. Lewis, *Sex After Sixty* (New York: Harper & Row, 1976), book jacket.

2. Martin A. Berezin, "Psychodynamic Considerations of Aging and the Aged." *American Journal of Psychiatry* (June 1972), 128:1483–1491.

3 Physical Changes

1. John Gunther, *Death Be Not Proud* (New York: Modern Library by arrangement with Harper & Row, 1953), pp. 166–168.

2. Colette, *La Maison de Claudine,* quoted in *Earthly Paradise,* an autobiography drawn from her lifetime writings, by Robert Phelps (New York: Farrar, Straus & Giroux, 1966), pp. 19–22.

3. American Heart Association, 44 East 23rd Street, New York, New York 10010. Pamphlet, *Heart of the Home.*

4. Lois Ellart, M.P.H., in cooperation with the Washtenaw County Council on Aging, Ann Arbor, Michigan, "Living Easy: Special Aids and Short Cuts for Independent Living." (Unpublished pamphlet.)

4 Personality Changes

1. Mark Jonathan Harris, "How to Pass the Test of Time," *New York Magazine,* January 17, 1977.

2. Dorothy Canfield Fisher, "Sex Education," included in *Insights: A Selection of Creative Literature About Children.* Selected and edited by the Child Study Association of America (New York: Jason Aronson, 1945).

3. Douglas V. Steere, *On Beginning from Within* (New York: Harper & Brothers, 1943), p. 135.

5 The Middle Generation

1. N. Kogan and M. A. Wallach, "Age Changes in Values and Attitudes," *Journal of Gerontology* (1961), 16:272.

2. Gail Sheehy, *Passages* (New York: E. P. Dutton & Co., 1976), pp. 258–259.

3. We are indebted to the writings of John Spiegel, M.D., Brandeis University, for the explanation of this theory.

7 When to Worry—and What to Do About It

1. L. S. Libow, "Pseudo-senility: Acute and Reversible Organic Brain Syndromes," *Journal of American Geriatrics Society* (March 1973), 21:112–120.

2. Richard Cohen, Washington *Post:* quoted in the Chicago *Sun-Times* "Living" section, June 11, 1978, p. 22.

3. Jacqueline Singer Edelson, "The Mentally Impaired Aged: Reordering Priorities," *Journal of Jewish Communal Service* (Fall 1976), 53, no. 1:63–73.

8 When It's Time to Say Goodbye

1. Steere, *On Beginning from Within,* p. 120.

2. Elizabeth Alexandra Bumagin died on July 22, 1977, at the age of twenty-four.

3. Laurence J. Peter and Raymond Hull, *The Peter Principle* (New York: Morrow, 1969).

4. Elisabeth Kübler-Ross, *On Death and Dying* (New York: Macmillan, paper edition, 1974), pp. 38–138.

5. Attributed to P. J. Macauley, newspaperman, father of a family friend.

6. Peter De Vries, *The Blood of the Lamb* (New York: Popular Library by arrangement with Little, Brown & Co., 1961), p. 179.

7. For further information, write to the Committee on the Treatment of Intractable Pain, Suite 302, 2001 S Street, N.W., Washington, D.C. 20009.

8. Sandol Stoddard, *The Hospice Movement* (New York: Stein & Day, 1978).

9. George and Helen Papashvily, *Anything Can Happen* (New York: Pocket Books, 1948), p. 177.

9 Death in the Family

1. Doris Lund, *Eric* (New York: Dell Publishing Co., 1975), p. 48.

Index